ARCHITECTURE ASIA

Journal of the Architects Regional Council Asia (ARCASIA)

Editorial Team

WU Jiang
Editor in Chief

LI Xiangning
Vice Editor in Chief

ZHOU Minghao
Managing Editor

WANG Ying
Executive Editor

WANG Yanze
Executive Editor

WEN Huajing
Assistant Editor

ZHENG Xin
Assistant Editor

Contact
archasia@foxmail.com

Co-Publishers

The Architectural Society of China (ASC)
9 Sanlihe Road, Beijing, China, 100835

Tongji University
1239 Siping Road, Shanghai, China, 200092

Sponsor

Tongji Architectural Design (Group) Co., Ltd.
1230 Siping Road, Shanghai, China, 200092

Editorial Board

Abu Sayeed M. Ahmed
University of Asia Pacific, Bangladesh
President of ARCASIA

Russell Dandeniya
RDC Architects, Sri Lanka
Vice President of Zone A, ARCASIA

Ana S. Mangalino-Ling
JSLA Architects, Philippines
Vice President of Zone B, ARCASIA

Chun Gyu Shin
CGS Architects and Associates, South Korea
Vice President of Zone C, ARCASIA

KONG Yuhang
Tianjin University, China
Appointee from publisher

CAO Jiaming
The Architectural Society of Shanghai, China
Appointee from publisher

WU Jiang
Tongji University, China
Editor in Chief

LI Xiangning
Tongji University, China
Vice Editor in Chief

Stefano BOERI
Politeconico in Milan, Italy
External advisor proposed by publisher, approved by ARCASIA

Advisory Board Members

Ashutosh Kr AGARWAL
Ashutosh Kr Agarwal Architects, India

BOON Che Wee
GRA Architects Sdn Bhd, Malaysia

CHANG Ping Hung
Hong Kong University, Hong Kong, China

Calvin CHUA
Spatial Anatomy, Singapore

Apurva Bose DUTTA
Independent writer, architecture journalist, editor, India

Kenneth FRAMPTON
Columbia University, USA

HENG Chye Kiang
National University of Singapore, Singapore

Hilde HEYNEN
University of Leuven, Belgium

Kazuo IWAMURA
Tokyo City University, Japan

Juwon KIM
Hongik School of Architecture, South Korea

Min Seok KIM
Notion Architecture, South Korea

George KUNIHIRO
Kokushikan University, Japan

LEE Chor Wah
Former editor in chief of *Architecture Asia* and *Architecture Malaysia*, Malaysia

Shiqiao LI
University of Virginia, USA

Peter ROWE
Harvard University, USA

Nabah Ali SAAD
Lahore Campus, Pakistan

Khadija Jamal SHABAN
Smart Project Development, Pakistan

Nuno SOARES
Urban Practice Ltd., Macau, China

TAN Beng Kiang
National University of Singapore, Singapore

WANG Jianguo
Southeast University, Academician of Chinese Academy of Engineering, China

Johannes WIDODO
National University of Singapore, Singapore

WONG Ying Fai
The Hong Kong Institute of Architects, Hong Kong, China

Charlie Qiuli XUE
City University of Hong Kong, Hong Kong, China

Jianfei ZHU
Newcastle University, UK

ZHUANG Weimin
Tsinghua University, Academician of Chinese Academy of Engineering, China

Contents

Editorial [3]

ARTICLE

The Collective Memory of a Chinese Community Survives in a Concrete Forest: "Chinatown" in Kuala Lumpur, Malaysia [4]
NG Shi Qi, GONG Xiaolei

How Does Street Art Affect a City's Social Identity? [16]
Rozanne Jojo VALLIVATTAM, Ramneet KAUR

An Investigation of Youth Homelessness and the Principles of Transitional Space Design [26]
ZHOU Kai, Greg MISSINGHAM

PROJECT

Kids Smile Labo Nursery [33]
Hibinosekkei, Youji no Shiro

Sukagawa Community Center [40]
Ishimoto Architectural & Engineering Firm, Unemori Architects

St. Andrews Institute of Technology and Management: Boys' Hostel Block [50]
Zero Energy Design Lab (ZED Lab)

St. Andrews Institute of Technology and Management: Girls' Hostel Block [55]
Zero Energy Design Lab (ZED Lab)

VORA (Vorasombat Plaza) [60]
SPACE | STORY | STUDIO

The Northstar School [67]
Shanmugam Associates

Tibet Intangible Cultural Heritage Museum [74]
Shenzhen Huahui Design Co., Ltd

Majiabang Cultural Museum [81]
Tongji Architectural Design (Group) Co. Ltd

Visitor Center of Changping Future Science City [88]
Huyue Studio

Morse Park Amphitheatre [96]
Architectural Services Department, HKSARG

Striated House at Rajagiriya [102]
Palinda Kannangara Architects

Editorial

Asian countries have different cultures, with various religions, traditions, and perceptions. Cultural identity is particularly important for regions and cities, where different groups of people live. Sense of identity is often related to nationality, ethnicity, religion, social class, generation, place of settlement, or even a social group with its unique culture. At the same time, whether based on homogeneous or heterogeneous cultures, social responsibility and social care are indispensable to maintain the balance between economic development and social welfare, and to remove barriers between people imposed by region, distance, economic conditions, and so on. The three articles in this issue take these ideas as a starting point for discussion.

Chinatown in Kuala Lumpur, Malaysia, carries the collective memory of the Chinese diaspora, which is often ignored in development and regeneration. Through examining past images and official blueprints of the area's layout, evaluating the spatial configuration in Chinatown, and reviewing the literature, Ng Shi Qi and Gong Xiaolei's article analyzes and evaluates the conceptual structural framework of the connections among the communities, place, and time that sustain the collective memory of a place and its influence. Rozanne Jojo Vallivattam and Ramneet Kaur's article examines how street art can affect a city's social identity, in terms of the parameters of location, physical attributes (color, design, and scale), user activities, and conception. To deal with the global issue of youth homelessness through social care, Zhou Kai and Greg Missingham's article identifies the principles of transitional space design by redefining how a shelter functions, and by considering how humanizing spatial design characteristics could create a more holistic solution.

Asian architectural practice started to explore cultural identity from a rising of national consciousness in the early twentieth century. With the modernization of social civilization, the responsibility of building Asian societies has been increasingly reflected in the development of architecture and cities; architecture plays an important role in cultural cohesion and transmission. From a nursery to school, the projects in this issue explore enlightenment of the new generation, from discipline to personality cultivation. From a museum to community center, they reflect various forms of cultural communication, from elite output to grassroots interaction. From a service facility to landscape architecture, they demonstrate the form transformation of urban spectacle in the public space. Architects from Japan, China, India, Thailand, and Sri Lanka keep on experimenting with space, structure, and materials, showing an infinite imagination of Asian wisdom in expressing the theme.

The Collective Memory of a Chinese Community Survives in a Concrete Forest: "Chinatown" in Kuala Lumpur, Malaysia

NG Shi Qi, Tianjin University, China
GONG Xiaolei* , Tianjin University, China

Abstract

"Chinatown" in Kuala Lumpur, Malaysia, was formed by the Chinese tin-mining community before Malaysia was established. It has managed to sustain its collective memory rooted in the past, while embracing widespread development in the country. This ongoing study investigates the survival of this collective memory under the pressure of regeneration. The research examines the conceptual framework of collective memory, which is influenced by the citizens and their surroundings, diachronicity, and synchronicity. The methodology comprises examining past images and official blueprints of the area's layout, evaluating the spatial configuration in Chinatown, and reviewing the literature. It is, therefore, crucial to analyze and evaluate the conceptual structural framework of the connections among the communities, place, and time that sustain the collective memory of a place and their influence, rather than turning them into a memorial that is frozen in time.

Author Information
NG Shi Qi: berry941@hotmail.com
GONG Xiaolei [*corresponding author]: gongxiaolei@tju.edu.cn

Keywords

Collective memory, spatial configuration, Chinatown, Chinese community, Kuala Lumpur.

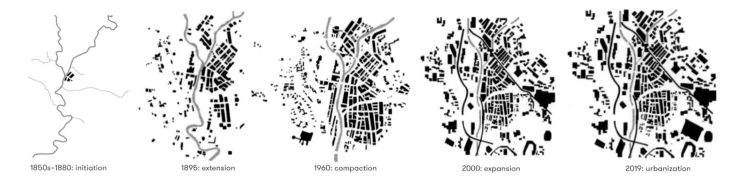

| 1850s–1880: initiation | 1895: extension | 1960: compaction | 2000: expansion | 2019: urbanization |

Figure 1
The changing topographies
of Kuala Lumpur beginning
in the 1850s

1. Introduction

Malaysia is a multiracial country comprising different languages, cultures, religions, types of fashion, and foods. The history of its capital city, Kuala Lumpur (KL), can be divided into several communities. The Malaysian Chinese, and British colonial seculars are represented along (and separated) by the Klang River, with the Indian community joining the area after to form little India. As communities developed, shophouses[1] were built to meet the functions of commercial and residential use and became common in South Asia. In Malaysia, the shophouses in Penang and Melaka are well-known, and in 2008, were recognized by UNESCO as a World Heritage Site. However, the shophouses in KL have received less attention. The research for this paper took place in KL's oldtown "Chinatown," which contains the majority of shophouses from the past, starting from 1895 (Figure 1)—the Chinese community zone has drastically expanded—to the early development of KL. Chinatown has witnessed the forming of Malaysia beginning during the British Malaya period[2] and, thus, offers a moment in time from which to begin examining the transformation and sustainability of the Chinese community's collective memory. Memory preserves and inherits past events that sustain it for the future. Hence, collective memory plays a crucial role on sense of belonging because it allows new generations to understand the past and their origins, and, thereby, reinforce this sense of belonging.

While several researchers have highlighted Chinatown in KL, they tend to mention the conservation and preservation of its historical buildings (for example, Petaling Street) and the lost and vanishing identity of its community, but not the collective memory of daily community life there. Chinatown is located in the downtown area of the city, with urbanization occurring right beside it, just outside its perimeter. In this research, we aim to analyze the site (Chinatown) and materialize its collective memory as a gathering spot of the Chinese community, to enhance the sustainability of the collective memory in the face of changes due to urbanization. This article does not address political, financial, conservation, or preservation issues in Malaysia.

The paper is divided into four parts: the history and background of Chinese immigrants and Chinatown in KL; the methodology, which uses urban planner Kevin Lynch's[3] constructs of "legibility" and "imageability" to come up with a spatial configuration of shophouses, circulation, and gray space in Chinatown, and the overlapping of the analysis map to examine collective memory in Chinatown; a discussion of "fading," "sharing," and "regeneration" in Chinatown; and a concluding discussion with suggestions for further research.

2. Background: The History of Chinatown in Kuala Lumpur

2.1 Migration of Chinese People
Chinese culture, language, food, religion, and customs have been maintained well by Chinese people in Malaysia, also known as Malaysian Chinese.[4] According to historical records, Chinese migrants started arriving in KL from the middle of the nineteenth century; most of them were Cantonese speakers from Southern China. The peak period of migration was from 1880 to 1940. Prior to this, most of the earliest Chinese migrants were merchants, though later, however, working in the Malaysian tin-mining industry became the main reason for Chinese people

5

migrating to Malaysia. In the past, the Chinese in Malaysia had dominated the rubber estates and tin mines, but during the British colonial period, the Chinese became more distributed toward business and tin mining.

2.2 Forming of Chinatown

Kuala Lumpur began as a small jetty at the junction of the Klang and Gombak rivers that were surrounded by jungle. In 1857, Rajah Abdullah, the chief of the capital of Klang, sent a party of eighty-seven Chinese prospectors on an expedition to look for potential tin-mining locations, which they found in Ampang, 2 miles from Klang. Chinese miners began to settle there (Figure 1, page 5) and the town expanded[5] and became known as Kuala Lumpur, or KL for short. Subsequently, the British moved their residency, including their government offices, from Klang to KL when they discovered that the natural landscape—particularly the Klang River— had the makings to potentially divide the community according to race, thereby better enabling them to control the area. Thus, they pushed the development of the city—such as the rail system to deliver goods from the Klang harbor to KL—and this cultural shift contributed to the vibrant city we see today. The river, by way of its very nature and course, separated the communities along it according to race and this helped shape the cultural transformation and rich architectural heritage styles of today that are noticed across this River of Life (RoL).[6]

In 1895, the colonial territory on the west bank was extended, as were the Malay enclave to the north and the Chinese settlement on the east bank, the three divided by the Klang and Gombak rivers (Figure 1, page 5). In 1960, development expanded to include the southern edge of the east bank—Brickfield area—which largely comprised the Indian community. It was also during this period that KL experienced a wave of uncontrolled development to accommodate the rise in migration to the city. In 2000, the traffic network expanded, crossing the parcel boundary; high-rise buildings were built, pushing the outskirts further to provide affordable housing for the growing population. Urbanization made more of the city accessible, as highways, railways, and public transport expanded, creating a node of juxtaposition where different architectural heritage elements are surrounded by the newer concrete forest.

There is no clear record of the origins of the name "Kuala Lumpur," but there are two common explanations:
1. It was translated from *lampang*, the Hakka word for "a muddy unclear forest;" and
2. It originates from the Malay word *kuala* meaning "the junction of two rivers," and the word *lumpur*, meaning "muddy."
Regardless of which is the more accurate version, both express the idea of a muddy river junction. The name continued to be used even during the British colonial era in Malaysia because the intention was to represent the power of two different races—Malay and Chinese—and retain "associationism with the native system"[7] rather than rename the new capital with an English name.

One man who cannot be ignored in discussions of Chinatown's development is Yap Ah Loy, the founding father of KL. He was the third captain of the Chinese[8] of the city from 1868 to 1885[9] and was the most powerful owner of a mining business in KL during that period. Additionally, he owned many of the shophouses along the Klang River and developed a large area of the land beside the Klang and Gombak Rivers. The community even named a street after him, and founded the Yap Clan

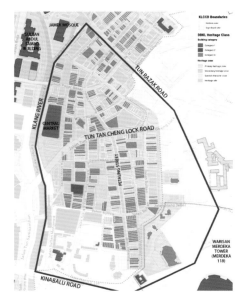

Figure 2
Chinatown in Kuala Lumpur

Figure 3
Building typology of Chinatown, Kuala Lumpur

Figure 4
Shophouses in Chinatown,
Kuala Lumpur

Association in his honor, and built the Kapitan Yap Ah Loy Memorial to memorialize his contributions.

2.3 Topology of Shophouses

According to Dewan Bandaraya Kuala Lumpur (DBKL)[10] Heritage Class,[11] Chinatown is in the historic area of KL and is categorized as a secondary heritage zone (Figure 2, page 6); a majority of the buildings are categorized as secondary class. Of the 393 building units in Chinatown, 152 are traditional shophouses and 241 are modern shophouses, which shows that shophouses comprise the majority of the area's building typology (Figure 3, page 6).

The construction of shophouses boomed during the mid-nineteenth century to meet the needs and demands of a growing society during the tin-mining period, specifically, the need for both business and residential spaces. In the early stages, the shophouses were constructed with two stories, and later, three stories, with the first floor used for retail purposes (primarily for the family business) and the upper floors for dwelling. Buildings were typically made of timber, with attap[12] used for the roof; all materials were gathered from the nearby jungle. However, after several destructive fires and floods, construction material gradually made the shift to the more durable brick. The fire of August 1872[13] was attributed to the close distance between the buildings, and another, in January 1881 (a flood also occurred in 1881), to the flammable building materials. To address these flaws, town planners of the British Colonial rule instituted a mandate to rebuild all timber shophouses and buildings with durable materials, construct a 5-foot-wide covered walkway[14] in front of the shophouses, and construct a back lane that allowed passage for the fire brigade and bullock carts collecting sewerage.[15]

Shophouse typologies in KL differ slightly from those in Penang and Melaka, owing to the relatively later influence of Western design in KL. Kuala Lumpur was part of the Federal Malay States (FMS),[16] which comprised Selangor, Perak, Negeri Sembilan, and Pahang; therefore, the names of the typologies are different. Shophouse were designed beginning the 1880s, in the Straits eclectic typology, which was very similar to the Straits Settlement (Penang)[17] typology, followed by the early FMS eclectic design when the British took over the administration. Thus, building façades on shophouses beginning the second period were ornamented with, and heavily influenced by European styles. By the 1920s to 1930s, the late FMS eclectic style emerged, when façade decorations reduced and evolved into a linear decoration style, and by the 1930s, the art deco style gained presence, with clean façades, vertical or horizontal lines, and the wide use of steel and glass.[18] Though the shophouses in KL's Chinatown have survived to date, they severely lacked maintenance through history, and have suffered great disrepair, owing to loose building regulations. Therefore, many shophouses have been renovated, demolished, or, disappointingly, even replaced by modern high-rise buildings. These actions have caused disorder in the urban fabric, building heights, and architectural elements.

3. Methodology

Several steps have been taken in this research project to analyze KL's Chinatown. Preliminary data was derived from reviewing the literature and collecting data from previous researches online, and from an ongoing site analysis in Chinatown using the "five elements" conceptualized by Lynch;[19] site analysis includes the shophouses and the gray space spatial configuration of

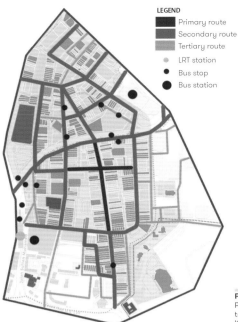

Figure 5
Pedestrian paths and public
transport in Chinatown,
Kuala Lumpur

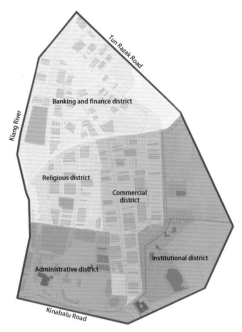

Figure 6
Edges and districts of
Chinatown, Kuala Lumpur

the shophouses in Chinatown. After collecting this data, we began overlapping the literature review results and other text-based data with the site analyses.

3.1 The "Five Elements" of Urban Space

We used Lynch's concepts of "legibility" and "imageability"[20] as they relate to cognition in urban spaces, and tracked and filtered the activities of the Chinese community and the area in which they live, to assess the formation of Chinese collective memory in Chinatown that happens apart from their relationship with historical buildings. Legibility represents the cognition of a user when in a given space, while imageability is a combination of information about one's environment and legibility.
Lynch describes the "five elements" of urban space this way: "Urban space that exists in a resident's perceptual 'imageability' as spatial elements and classification standards for environmental assessment are paths, edges, districts, nodes, and landmarks." Of course, collective memory is constructible and sustainable, therefore, as researchers, we not only focus on the long-term resident, but also on the newer generations. Memory can only be shared with the involvement of new input.

Paths are the routes that residents take as they move around by walking, driving, or taking public transport. In this analysis, the path focuses on pedestrian and public transport modes because it is preferable to navigate Chinatown by walking, and public transport is convenient—parking is difficult and several areas are pedestrian-only, such as Petaling Street (Ci Chang Street) and back lanes with mural paintings. The primary pedestrian route follows Petaling Street (Ci Chang Street);

the secondary route goes along the main road and is the way to reach locations such as the public transport station; the tertiary route mainly consists of the back lanes behind shophouses and other buildings (Figure 5).

The edges of Chinatown form the East bank of the Klang River, all the way to the bottom of Kinabalu Road and the side highway, Tun Razak Road (Figure 6). The Tun Tan Cheng Lock Road that crosses Chinatown has separated it into top and bottom areas; the top, which is the banking area, consists of late-style shophouses and modernized buildings, while the bottom part consists buildings that feature the early shophouse typology, as well as local businesses.

Adding to this, Chinatown is divided into five district areas (Figure 6) based on their predominant use: the banking and finance district comprises the top part of Chinatown in the figure and it's closer to the center of the oldtown; the religious district is on the left side, where Chinese and Hindu temples are located; the commercial district that includes Petaling Street (Ci Chang Street) is located in the center of Chinatown and is easy to approach from other districts; the administrative district is located at the bottom left of Chinatown and includes the police station; and the institutional district, where dialect halls are located, is on the right side of Chinatown.

Nodes in Chinatown can be categorized into two types: point and linear (Figure 7, page 9). Point nodes are primarily road junctions where pedestrians stop and cross over a road, public transport junctions, and open space in the financial district. Linear nodes are the Kasturi Walk, Petaling Street (Ci Chang Street), Penjaja Gallery (wet market and food court), and Panggung Street (Kwai Chai Hong), all of which are pedestrian-only walkways.

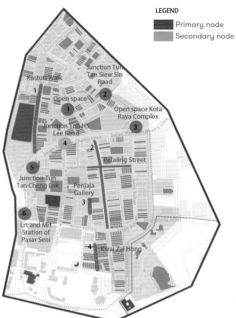

Figure 7
Nodes in Chinatown,
Kuala Lumpur

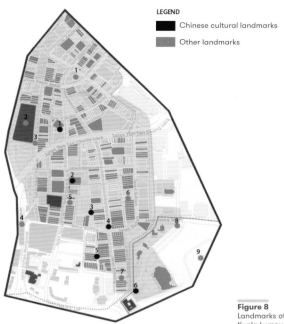

Figure 8
Landmarks of Chinatown,
Kuala Lumpur

Among the linear node, Kasturi Walk and Petaling Street (Ci Chang Street) have been official tourist spots for some time now, while Panggung Street (Kwai Chai Hong) is the latest tourist attraction, and is also visited by many locals. The Penjaja Gallery, however, is visited mainly by locals only because it is a wet market and food court with cheaper food, and is adjacent to an open carpark (which is a private carpark that charges by the hour).

In addition to these elements, landmarks play an important role in urban space cognition because they can act as a reference point defined by something other than the height of the building, according to Lynch. In this project, we categorize landmarks into "Chinese cultural landmarks" and "other landmarks" (Figure 8). The Chinese cultural landmarks consist of: Sin Sze Ya Temple (No. 1 on the map in Figure 8), Guan Ti Temple (No. 2), Penjaja Gallery entrance (No. 3), Petaling Street (Ci Chang Street) gate (No. 4), Panggung Street (Kwai Chai Hong) mural painting (No. 5), and Chen Shi Shu Yuan (No. 6). The other landmarks are: Klang bus station (No. 1), Central Market (No. 2), Kasturi Walk entrance with its *wau* (or "kite") design (No. 3), Pasar Seni LRT (No. 4), Sri Maha Mariamman Temple (a Hindu temple) (No. 5), Pasar Karat mural painting (No. 6), blacksmith mural painting (No. 7), a gospel church (No. 8), and Merdeka 118, which is still under construction (No. 9).

3.2 Spatial Configuration of Chinatown
A spatial configuration analysis covers Chinatown's urban planning for the shophouse area, circulation, and gray space. While the spatial configuration of community gathering spots in Chinatown can be narrowed, filtered, and analyzed, the results would not represent the collective memory of Chinatown, if we don't also examine the relationship between the gray spaces and

the rest of the community, an essential aspect for sustaining the collective memory of the Chinese community. This is especially true, given the development that Chinatown has undergone, and continues to undergo, which has included the replacement of some areas in Chinatown with a new collective memory that has been formed without the Chinese community.

The selection of the shophouse will be narrowed down according to traditional and modern shophouses, as delineated in Figure 3 (page 6). Circulation is divided into four categories: the main public route, the secondary route, the tertiary roads, and the back lanes. Gray space is concentrated in the top part, around the central market (where the homeless "camp"), in the green area beside the banking district (residential), in the Petaling Street (Ci Chang Street) tourist hotspots (where the homeless "camp"), and at Sultan Road and Panggung Street (residential) in the bottom area of Chinatown.[21]

4. Discussion

The results from our analysis of Chinatown are divided into three parts: "fading"—which refers to the huge change of the urban fabric that has transformed the function to the needs of the present day, and the disappearing of the daily life of the Chinese community, "sharing"—the places that manage to sustain the collective memory without much changes from the current situation, and "regeneration"—which refers to the area experiencing changes, but at the same time, there are new projects or buildings trying to bring back the collective memory of the Chinese community and sustain it (Figure 10, page 10). These perspectives are intended to raise

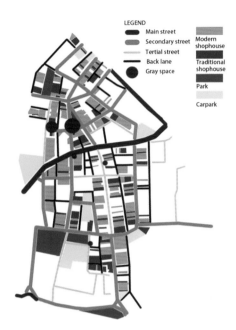

LEGEND
- Main street
- Secondary street
- Tertial street
- Back lane
- Gray space

Modern shophouse
Traditional shophouse
Park
Carpark

Figure 9
Spatial configuration of shophouses, circulation, and gray space in Chinatown, Kuala Lumpur

Figure 10
Overlapping analyses of Chinatown in Kuala Lumpur

Figure 11
Fading of Chinatown's collective memory

Figure 12
At the entrance to Petaling Street (Ci Chang Street) in Chinatown, Kuala Lumpur

Figure 13
Sharing collective memory in Chinatown, Kuala Lumpur

awareness of the possibilities for, and the challenges that face the future of Chinatown, and thus stimulate examination of the diachronicity and synchronicity of Chinatown, and the relationships among the place, community, and time.

4.1 Fading of the Collective Memory

The fading of the collective memory began when the contribution of Yap Ah Loy was replaced by Raja Abdullah,[22] who was then (in 1857) presented as the founder of Kuala Lumpur. This narrative was accepted by the History Association of Federal Territory[23] and subsequently, taught and disseminated through official school textbooks.[24]

Apart from that, the replacement of Chinese road names in KL also erases the memory of the Chinese community because "the naming of streets, roads, and places (plays) an important role in making a place".[25] Naming a road after a person acknowledges that person's contributions to the area. However, Chinatown today is left with only four Chinese road names: Yap Ah Loy Road, Tun Tan Cheng Lock Road, Tan Siew Sin Road, and Tun H. S. Lee Road (Figure 11, page 10); the replacement of road names happened in other places in KL as well.

The Petaling Street (Ci Chang Street) pedestrian shopping mall project has been successful in becoming a popular tourist venue, but it is also a space connected with a sad memory for the Chinese community in KL. The current Petaling Street (Ci Chang Street) used to be Ci Chang Street and was considered the most important street—as the central place of business, culture, education, and religion. Ci Chang Street ("茨厂街" or *Ci Chang Jie*) (Figure 12, page 10) was named after a tapioca-processing factory owned by Yap Ah Loy. The local Chinese community has

Figure 14
Mural paintings in Panggung Street (Kwai Chai Hong), Kuala Lumpur

always preferred the name "Ci Chang Street," however, "Petaling Street (Ci Chang Street)" is favored by the government, tourists, and other races. Despite the resistance of the Chinese community to the new name, nothing can be done, except to simply use the area's original name within the Chinese community when referring to the street. It can also be seen in this area that traditional businesses have been replaced by those selling cheap counterfeits and knock-offs, and pirated goods, blemishing Chinatown with a fake image—ironically, presenting grand Chinese feature gates at the front, and at the end of Petaling Street (Ci Chang Street), allowing the ousting of local stall owners by non-Chinese foreign workers that sell pirated stuff. There is little interaction among the developer and community, in turn causing many locals to move out from Chinatown.

Another example of fading is seen in the Central Market, built in 1888 by Yap Ah Loy to provide a wet market. This space is now a tourist spot and the wet market of the Chinese community has been moved to the back lane of Tun H. S. Lee Road, Penjaja Gallery. Pork was banned when the Central Market became a tourist venue, given that the function of the once wet market had changed, and also because Malaysia is officially a Muslim country, where Muslims, by religion, must only consume halal food, which does not permit the consumption of pork. However, pork was (and is) a daily food for the Chinese community and so they had to build themselves a wet market that was non-halal.[26]

The naming of Chinatown in 2003 rejected the contributions and efforts of the Chinese community that have been made from the Malaya period to current day. The "Chinatown" concept is used mainly by Western countries as a reference tag to describe the ethnic minority space in which primarily Chinese businesses and restaurants, and Chinese immigrants exist, within an otherwise non-Chinese population. The Chinese population in Malaysia is the second largest population; it has reduced, decreasing from 38 percent in 1947[27] to 22.6 percent in 2021.[28] Malaysia has officially accepted the Chinese community, yet, in what can be inferred as poor taste that hints at informal ostracism, named the area where KL's Chinese community had sprung up and established roots in as "China" town.

The shophouses that have historical value are located around the center and the bottom boundary of Chinatown (Figure 12, page 10). The sustainability of the collective memory occurs mainly in those areas, within the buildings from the past that echo those memories. Many shophouses have been demolished and replaced with modern, taller shophouses that have more stories to accommodate the current demands of urbanization. The banking and finance district, too, will gradually fade away, as the building typology and land use are transformed substantially to serve urbanization, and the gray space in which the homeless gather has become an area that the community avoids.

Some family businesses have been forced to close, to be replaced by trendy shops that cater to tourists. The community's collective identity and memory are declining slowly, tearing bit by bit, without the younger generation's awareness of the older generations' efforts.

4.2 Sharing

Sharing and sustaining collective memory happens mainly in the areas indicated in Figure 13 (page 11). The back lanes were historically the areas where the community gathered and where children played; however, those activities have largely vanished

Figure 15
Regeneration in Chinatown,
Kuala Lumpur

Figure 16
Merdeka 118 looming behind
Chinatown in Kuala Lumpur

from those areas since the current back lanes were transformed into service lanes and parking zones. Interestingly, some of these activities have continued on side streets and back lanes, such as in the extension of Petaling Street (Ci Chang Street)—in front of shophouses, Penjaja Gallery, and Panggung Street (Kwai Chai Hong), all of which are located beside or behind the shophouses (Figure 13, page 11). Therefore, while the impact on back lanes has been reduced by the shifting of these activities, the change has caused the homeless to gather in nearby areas such as corridors in front of abandoned shophouses, instead of the back lanes.

Chinatown adapts to the changes in the city and, in turn, avoids elimination in the present era. Indeed, some adaptive reuse projects have upgraded the interiors of shophouses and maintained the original façade features, which has successfully brought back the young generation to these spaces. One example is Ho Kaw Hainan Kopitiam; the owner often animatedly shares his memories of the past community with diners who arrive after peak hours, when he has free moments to engage with his customers.

Another subject of contest among the Chinese community in Chinatown is the project in Panggung Street, also known as Kwai Chai Hong ("鬼仔巷"or *Gui Zai Xiang*) by Think City.[29] They argued against the project because it actually brought back negative images from the past, compared to the more positive images of the other streets. According to the locals, the street was notorious as a venue for solicitation, lined with brothels frequented by male clientele, and where street workers waited for Western customers. The name of the street actually originates from a colloquial slang referring to the many children born there with Western fathers. In the daytime, the children played by the road, and have now become a representative image of that place in Chinatown. Even though the

site presents the negative history of the Chinese community, the community manages to remember both the good and the bad aspects of the past. There are also many murals in the street; one can listen to a soundtrack, which plays when they scan the code beside the mural painting, to connect with stories of the past. The street echoes its memory through paintings of the everyday life of the past (Figure 14, page 11), and through collaborating with several food and beverage shops to attract customers to the area, thereby making effort to save the dying businesses in the street.

4.3 Regeneration

The regeneration of KL's Chinatown is also seen in the site analysis and the development blueprint of Kuala Lumpur (Figure 15, page 12).

The updating of KL's Mass Rapid Transit (MRT)[30] system, as part of its public transit network, connects Chinatown to other areas, which is especially convenient for visitors. The MRT connection has made transportation around KL convenient, and linked areas that are not served by Keretapi Tanah Melayu Berhad (KTM)[31] or the Light Rail Transit (LRT) links.

The analysis map also shows that the urbanization border is getting closer to Chinatown, situated just a a street distance away (right behind Chinatown), with Merdeka 118, which will be completed in 2022, and which will be the tallest building in Malaysia. On the one hand, this new development provides opportunities for Chinatown because it can bring more financial support to the old local shops and thus, it can be an opportunity to spread a good image of the Chinese community in that area. On the other hand, it raises challenges, such as the fading collective memory of the community, while inserting new memory for the future that might not at all relate to the local Chinese community,

13

Figure 17
Petaling Street (Ci Chang Street) in the past

because developers often target old shophouses for modern redevelopment and trendy tourist-centered businesses. Additionally, the huge contrast between Chinatown and the surrounding area is being exacerbated by the construction of buildings like Merdeka 118 (Figure 16), which is located just beyond Chinatown's border.

It should be noted that, while the city is still in the process of development, many shophouses remain in a demolished state, and still many others are on the verge of ruin, displaying only sad remnants of the glory of the past era; no actions have been taken by owners, authority figures, or developers to address this situation.

The Draft Kuala Lumpur Structure Plan 2040[32] includes several proposals for Chinatown, such as administering its planning as part of KL's creative economy, culture, and tourism landmark. For example, the new connecting links between the RoL (new tourist zones) and the Central Market (cultural zone); the revitalization of Central Market and Medan Pasar; and the improvement of cultural areas, such as upgrading Sin Sze Si Ya Temple and Petaling Street (Ci Chang Street) with new open-gallery display centers by reusing empty space around Panggung Street and reactivating ground-floor business in Chinatown to attract tourists and reinforce the creative and cultural district.

Undeniably, the site analysis is disadvantaged without the ability to gather quantitative data (such as age, race, accessibility, and job occupation) of Chinatown's citizens who interact with its physical spaces.

5. Conclusion

Chinatown in KL presently serves a purpose that is not conducive to remembering and sustaining the Chinese community. The present research observeds that the pedestrian street market layout is similar, diachronically, to the shophouses— that is, the market stalls are similar to the shophouses, but have different commercial purposes, and the path between the stalls is similar to the 5-foot walkways that connect the shophouses.

Petaling Street (Ci Chang Street) has been sustaining the street market environment since the past (Figure 17).

However, from a synchronic perspective, it is observed: The wet market has been moved from Central Market to Penjaja Gallery; gathering spots have transitioned from the back lanes to coffeeshops and the 5-foot walkways in front of the shophouses; and the traditional education system has been replaced with the standard school system. Further, temporal changes can be seen in the land use and building typology, from business-and-living units to the present commercial area, in the migration of the Chinese community out of Chinatown, in the vanishing of the old commercial area in Petaling Street (Ci Chang Street) and its transformation into a pedestrian shopping mall for tourism, and in the replacement of family businesses with financial buildings and trendy businesses to meet tourism demands.

The relationships among place, community, and time perform different important roles in the sustainability of collective memory. The local Chinese community is the subject that must maintain and sustain its collective memory, while shophouses and the back lanes of Chinatown are the objects of that memory, and old photos, story sharing, and mural paintings have become the carrier of that memory.

The site analyses in this article cannot fully represent the collective memory, but we will continue to examine the material and the continuing aspects of the collective memory. Importantly, this analysis provides a foundation for understanding the local Chinese community in KL's Chinatown from a historical and spatial configuration perspective. This article does not intend to address race issues, it examines the spaces of the current Chinatown through the separate lenses of "fading," "sharing," and "regeneration" in an effort to preserve and maintain its roots and raise awareness among the younger Chinese community. The younger Chinese generations may lack a sense of cultural awareness and belonging because they have missed the platform and connectivity to the origins of their Chinese community in Kuala Lumpur.

"The place of memory exists only in the interaction between memory and history."[33]

Acknowledgment

This paper is an output of a project that is a part of an ongoing Master's thesis.

Notes

1. Shophouses are a building type that combines the commercial space on the first floor with a residence on the upper floor. Shophouses can be found in Southeast Asia and they are usually built in a row.
2. The British Malaya period or "*Tanah Melayu British*" in Malay. It refers to when the Malay Peninsula and Singapore were under the British government, between the late-eighteenth and the mid-twentieth centuries.
3. Kevin Lynch, *The Image of the City* (Cambridge, MA: MIT Press, 2012), https://www.miguelangelmartinez.net/IMG/pdf/1960_Kevin_Lynch_The_Image_of_The_City_book.pdf.
4. "Malaysian Chinese," Wikipedia, last modified January 1, 2022, https://en.wikipedia.org/wiki/Malaysian_Chinese.
5. "History of Kuala Lumpur," Visit KL, official tourism portal of the city, http://www.visitkl.gov.my/visitklv2/index.php?r=column/cone&id=6.
6. "RoL" or the "River of Life" project falls under the government's Economic Transformation Program, and aims to transform the Klang River into a waterfront with high economic value.
7. Yat Ming Loo, "The Making of 'Chinatown'," in *Architecture and Urban Form in Kuala Lumpur: Race and Chinese Spaces in a Postcolonial City* (London: Routledge, 2016), 109–144.
8. Captain of the Chinese, normally addressed as *Kapitan Cina* or *Kapitan China* in Malay. It is a position that is in charge of the Chinese community.
9. "Yap Ah Loy," Academic Dictionaries and Encyclopedias, 2010, https://en-academic.com/dic.nsf/enwiki/855497.
10. Dewan Bandaraya Kuala Lumpur (DBKL) is also known as Kuala Lumpur City Hall, which administers the city of KL; it was established after KL was officially granted city status on February 1, 1972.
11. The Heritage Class by DBKL divides the city into building categories and heritage zones for cultural buildings or sites according to DBKL guidelines.
12. Attap is named after the attap palm, which is commonly used for traditional housing, particularly to build roofs, in village areas.
13. Nadiyanti Mat Nayan, "Conservation of Heritage Curtilages in Kuala Lumpur, Malaysia," PhD dissertation, University of Adelaide, July 2017: 11–42.
14. The "5-foot walkway," known as *kaki lima* in Malay and *wu jiao ji* (五脚基) in Mandarin refers to the covered sidewalks and corridors in front of the shophouses, which provide shelter from the sun and rain.
15. Wan Hashimah, Wan Ismail, and Hui Ching Low, "Back Lanes as Social Spaces in Chinatown, Kuala Lumpur," *Environment–Behavior Proceedings Journal* 1, no. 3 (August 2016): 293.
16. Federal Malay States (FMS) was established by the British government from 1896 to 1946.
17. The Straits Settlement was established by the British government and it refers to Penang, Dinding, Malacca (now Melaka), and Singapore.
18. "Old Shophouse of Kuala Lumpur," Walkabout Asia, YouTube, March 2, 2020, https://www.youtube.com/watch?v=XXVOEQI0gYA&ab_channel=WalkaboutAsia.
19. Kevin Lynch, *The Image of the City*.
20. ibid.
21. Uta Dietrich, "Homelessness in Kuala Lumpur," Think City website, May 8, 2018, https://thinkcity.com.my/wp-content/uploads/2019/09/Homelessness-Report-Final-07-May-2018.pdf.
22. Raja Abdullah was the representative of the Yam Tuan who administered Klang, and a member of the Selangor royal family, which formed KL in 1857 when he set out exploring the area for tin ore with eighty-seven Chinese workers.
23. The Federal Territory is called Wilayah Persekutuan in Malay and comprises KL, Labuan, and Putrajaya territories. They are governed directly by the Federal Government of Malaysia.
24. Yat Ming Loo, "The Making of 'Chinatown'."
25. ibid.
26. Halal or halal certification refers to consumables that are permissible for an Islamic country.
27. Charles Hirschman, "Demographic Trends in Peninsular Malaysia," *Population and Development Review* 6, no. 1 (March, 1980): 103–125, https://doi.org/10.2307/1972660.
28. "Demographic Statistic Third Quarter 2021, Malaysia," Department of Statistic Malaysia, official portal, released November 8, 2021, https://www.dosm.gov.my/v1/index.php?r=column/cthemeByCat&cat=430&bul_id=N05ydDRXR1BJWVITdDY4TldHd253dz09&menu_id=L0pheU43NWJwRWVSZklWdzQ4TlhUUT09.
29. Think City evolved from a city-making organizational aim to change the planned and developed city.
30. The MRT or Mass Rapid Transit serves to strengthen the rail transit network.
31. KTM was built during the British colonial era for tin transportation.
32. The Draft Kuala Lumpur Structure Plan 2040 contains the vision, goals, policies, and proposals for the development of Kuala Lumpur for the next twenty years. "Draft Kuala Lumpur Structure Plan, A City for All," Laman Web Rasmi Pelan Pembangunan Kuala Lumpur 2040, https://www.dbkl.gov.my/klmycity2040/?page_id=4304.
33. Pascal Moliner and Inna Bovina, "Architectural Forms of Collective Memory," *International Review of Social Psychology* 1, no. 12 (2019), http://doi.org/10.5334/irsp.236.

Figure Credits

Figure 1: The changing topographies of Kuala Lumpur: 1850, 1895, 1960, 2000, and 2019 (1850—"Kuala Lumpur Creative and Cultural District Strategic Master Plan," Think City, https://thinkcity.com.my/publications/KLCCD-Strategic-Masterplan-EN/#page=28; 1895, 1960, 2000, and 2019 —"Tales of Three Cities," Taylor's University, Slideshare, October 20, 2019, https://www.slideshare.net/Yuan0623/tales-of-three-cities-184191070).
Figure 2: Chinatown in Kuala Lumpur ("Categories of Heritage Buildings," Think City, authors' photo).
Figure 3: Building typology of Chinatown, Kuala Lumpur ("Architectural Styles of Heritage and Modern Buildings in Chinatown, Kuala Lumpur," Think City).
Figure 4: Shophouses in Chinatown, Kuala Lumpur (Wikimedia Commons).
Figure 5: Pedestrian paths and public transport in Chinatown, Kuala Lumpur (authors' image).
Figure 6: Edges and districts of Chinatown, Kuala Lumpur (authors' image).
Figure 7: Nodes in Chinatown, Kuala Lumpur (authors' image).
Figure 8: Landmarks of Chinatown, Kuala Lumpur (authors' image).
Figure 9: Spatial configuration of shophouses, circulation, and gray space in Chinatown, Kuala Lumpur (authors' image).
Figure 10: Overlapping analyses of Chinatown in Kuala Lumpur (authors' image).
Figure 11: Fading of Chinatown's collective memory (authors' image).
Figure 12: At the entrance to Petaling Street (Ci Chang Street) in Chinatown, Kuala Lumpur (WordPress, Petaling Street: Architecture, Cheah Ee Von).
Figure 13: Sharing collective memory in Chinatown, Kuala Lumpur (authors' image).
Figure 14: Mural paintings in Panggung Street (authors' photos).
Figure 15: Regeneration in Chinatown, Kuala Lumpur (authors' image).
Figure 16: Merdeka 118 looming behind Chinatown in Kuala Lumpur (authors' photo).
Figure 17: Petaling Street (Ci Chang Street) in the past from Teoh Chee Keong, *The Disappearing Kuala Lumpur* (Selangor, Mentor Publishing Sdn Bhd, 2012, 22).

How Does Street Art Affect a City's Social Identity?

Rozanne Jojo VALLIVATTAM, Atkins GTC
Ramneet KAUR, School of Planning and Architecture (SPA New Delhi), India

Abstract

Street art is a means of expression, through which artists seek to convey a message or express themselves. Each artist has their own unique style, which they project through their art to interact with the street and its occupants. This research paper examines the extent to which street art can affect a city's social identity, in terms of the following parameters: location, physical attributes (color, design, and scale), user activities, and conception. This study seeks to improve our understanding of the relationship between street art, the street, and its occupants. Artists who create street art aim to bring about a change in that space, as well as how people interact with that space. This study seeks to determine the precise parameters through which this change is brought about, and how they can be used to shift the functionality of a space, and thereby change its identity.

Author Information
Rozanne Jojo VALLIVATTAM: rozannejojo@gmail.com, ORCiD: 0000-0001-8707-3795
Ramneet KAUR: ar.ramneetkaur@gmail.com, ORCiD: 0000-0002-0410-9439

Keywords

Street art, social identity, location, physical attributes, user activity.

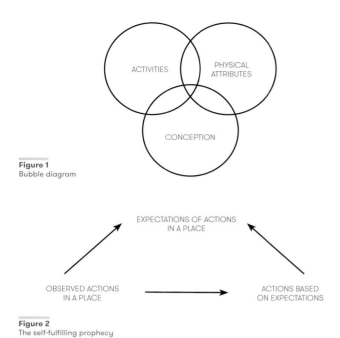

Figure 1
Bubble diagram

Figure 2
The self-fulfilling prophecy
of place/activities

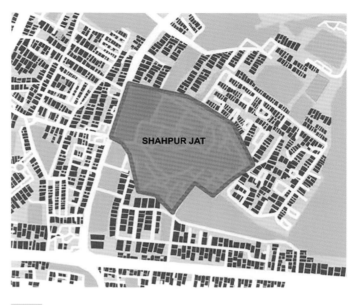

Figure 3
Plan view of Shahpur Jat

1. Introduction

Graffiti or street art is generally described as any form of
unsanctioned art in public or privately owned spaces.[1] It aims to
create a shift in the identity of the space and break the monotony
of the lives of normal city dwellers. Street art and graffiti are
usually exhibited throughout a city in the form of tags, sculptures,
stenciling, sticker art, street installations, and so on. All forms of
public art, ranging from street art to 3D installations, fall under
the category of urban art. The various types of urban art are
explained below.
· Street art/graffiti/spray painting: the most traditional form of
  street art is to paint directly on a property's surface.
· Stencil art: rather than using paintbrushes or rollers to paint the
  surfaces, stencils are used to make the process faster.
· Video projection: public art is created by screening visuals on a
  screen or wall to create a better-looking space.
· Street installation: these differ from conventional street art, as
  they utilize the 3D realm and project into the urban environment.
   This study focuses mainly on traditional street art. It should be
noted that street art and graffiti are, in fact, two different forms of
urban art, but the terms are treated as interchangeable in the
Indian context.
   Art is an evolutionary expression. The shape of art and its role in
society are constantly changing. At no point is art static, there are
no rules.[2] Through street art, an artist intends to bring about a
difference in society, whether in the form of spreading awareness,
shaping the general public's ideologies, or even bringing about a
change in the physicality and quality of a space, thus contributing
to the personality and identity of the city. This is done by

connecting the street through street art, making people aware of
their surroundings, and forcing them to look up and interact with
the space around them. It creates a dialogue between the public
and the artwork, allowing people to interact with the space. Unlike
paintings displayed in art galleries that are aimed at a certain
group of people, street art focuses more on the general public.
Street art is viewed by audiences of all ages, groups, and classes,
and is intended to be shared among a larger crowd. One
individual's response to a piece need not be the same as another's.
How a group of people interacts with a piece may not be the same
as how a single individual would, or how it would be received by
society in general, meaning that there are bound to be differences
in the reception of a piece. Each space has a different character
that evokes a different type of response from its audience, and this
in turn changes the character of the space. This concept can be
used to revive dead-end spaces by fostering activity and giving the
space a sense of character.
   This study investigates how street art can bring about a change
in the quality of a space and seeks to determine the parameters
that define this impact, whether positive or negative. It critically
analyzes how a space is affected, and examines how this can be
used to shape or change the identity of public spaces.

2. What are the Parameters That Define a Space's Social Identity?

Cities are manifestations of peoples' cultures and traditions,
historical periods, regions, environments, and climates. Therefore, a
city and its architecture have an unbroken relationship with
the culture of a society and people's lives, and changes in
them often accompany changes in lifestyle, views, and art.[3]

Figure 4
Street section sketches of
Shahpur Jat, Delhi

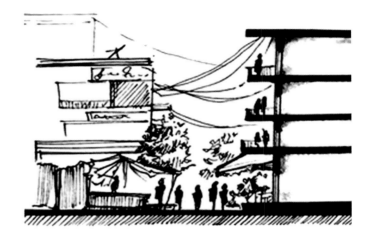

The fabric of a city that displays its identity and character at a macro level is closely linked to its culture and traditions. On a micro level, however, it is defined by the public interaction of the various groups of people that make up that space and use it. These aspects are well defined in David Canter's book, *The Psychology of Place*, which states that a place is a result of relationships between actions, conceptions, and physical attributes. It follows that place is defined by:
· behaviors associated with, anticipated in, or housed in a place;
· the setting's physical parameters; and
· conceptions that people have of those behaviors in that physical environment (Figure 1, page 17).

Characteristic spatial qualities can strengthen the image of particular paths. In the simplest sense, streets that suggest extremes in either width or narrowness attract attention;[4] as these streets grab more attention, they stimulate vigorous human interaction, creating an active space. In this way, the physical aspect of a space gives rise to a change in its social aspect. Elements that influence the social aspect of a space can be utilized to bring about a change in it, such as by enhancing the social quality of a space.

To describe a place, it is necessary to identify the people who use that area, their conceptions of the place, and their activities within it.[5] A space's identity is, therefore, not merely the outcome of its physical attributes, it is also contributed by the result of the activities revolving around the space, as well as the conceptions of the place embedded in people's minds.

Some places appear to have very specific functions and appropriate different categories of behavior, while others are more difficult to pin down. Their characters derive from the

Figure 5
The famous "Cat Painting" by Anpu Varkey in Shahpur Jat

range of behaviors they accommodate.[6] The description of a place is not based purely on its physical attributes, but largely on the activities and behaviors of the people occupying that space. Hence, we can conclude that it is mainly the people and behavioral activities surrounding a place that tailor a space's preconceived impression, in the process, giving it an identity. The differences between the various "user groups" play a vital role in instigating the various activities that eventually surround an area. Hence, the expectations of a place due to preconceived impressions, result in certain types of actions. This is described as part of a "self-fulfilling prophecy" by Canter in *The Psychology of Place* (Figure 2, page 17). Thus, what a place's identity becomes, depends largely on what people want to make of that space.

As we can see, a space's physical attributes create its character, which leads to actions based on expectations and, thus, also to its identity. This gives rise to important parameters, such as:
· location—context, and cultural and historical backgrounds;
· physical attributes—scale, color, and design;
· user activity—study done before and after incorporation of street art, if any; and
· conception—idea and image of the space

This study investigates the use of urban art as an element to shift the physicality of a space and hence bring about a change in the social realm. It further analyzes how urban art can be used as a landscaping element to create a shift in the identity of public spaces.

2.1 Does Street Art Transform the Physicality of a Space?

One simple way that street art can create a small change in the way people see a space is through the simple use of color. Psychological studies have demonstrated that color plays a significant role in people's moods and behaviors. It can create either a positive or a negative mood within someone, thus affecting their day-to-day functioning.

The Let's Color Program is built on a triple foundation: having a positive impact and inspiring the lives of the people in the communities, driving employee engagement, and building brands.[7] It is a globally known project that aims to bring communities together by using walls as bridges to connect people and spaces rather than divide them. It plays around with different colors that evoke different emotions, and hence varying reactions, from the public, thus transforming the character of a space. The project has showcased this principle through various experiments such as the "Double Staircase Experiment," in which a group of artists selected an indoor space that contained two sets of stairs that were equally used. One was painted in bright, vibrant colors, while the other was left as it was. It was observed that people were more inclined to use the set of stairs that had been painted, compared to the non-painted one. There was a change in the mood and behavior of the users as they ascended and descended the stairs. This method is now used by street artists all over the world, with abandoned spaces being renovated by adding bright, vibrant colors to them, giving them character. This, in turn, increases the number of people interacting with the space, giving it a certain identity. Another such experiment conducted by the Let's Color Program is the "Escalator Experiment" that was organized in an outdoor public space, where there was an escalator and a flight of stairs located side-by-side. Initially, it was observed that people preferred to use the escalator over the stairs because it was more convenient. Later,

the flight of stairs was painted in bright, vibrant colors to see if this would bring about any behavioral change among the public, and it did. More people started using the stairs instead, as they were fascinated by the vibrant colors. This changed the way people interacted with the space, and it was ultimately observed that 63 percent more people used the stairs than the escalator.

From this, we can infer that giving a space simple, bright colors can brighten it up and create changes in people's behavioral patterns and mindsets, shifting the conception of the space. This creates a shift in the identity of the space, but it does not change the space's main function. It does, however, increase the activities that take place in and around the space, allowing it to become a more active public node. In this manner, unused spaces can be brought back into a city's main urban fabric by evoking a conversation between the public and the space through the simple use of colors.

2.2 Does Street Art Impact the Social Realm?

Street art is not only used to enhance the quality of a space, but also to define its personality. What a space featuring street art becomes depends on how people interact with it through the reception of that street art. Thus, social interaction with the space plays a huge role in the way the space unravels. Street art has an impact on both the micro and macro levels of society and it aims to use this as a way to redefine a city, as well as perhaps improve it.

In Rio de Janeiro, for example, street art developed into a movement. It exists in all corners of the city, from upper-class neighborhoods to residential places and institutions. Street art only began to be taken seriously when it was legalized in March 2009.[8] Only then did Rio's artists begin to sculpt the urban landscape. Street art is now being used as an element to enhance the quality of public spaces and to portray the culture of the space. This has led to an evolution of the landscape in Brazil, and an emerging and divergent movement in the global street art landscape. Street art has been defined as the main landscaping element, paving a new path for landscape architecture; the colors have brought life to various spaces that were once abandoned. This has added to the landscape of the streets and given the spaces character and identity. Through street art, people are made aware of such spaces and are motivated to keep them clean and maintain them. In this way, street art contributes to keeping the city well maintained and helps bring discipline to people's behavior within it.

Street art was used in Rio de Janeiro as the main strategy to shape the social sphere and to change the city's identity. It was used as a landscaping element to enhance the beauty of the space and as a means of expressing and improving social welfare. From there, it became a method for establishing various areas of engagement and creating new, informal public spaces that allow interaction between residents and their city. This example shows how street art can be used as a landscaping element to activate spaces and create active public nodes.

3. Primary Case Studies

3.1 Shahpur Jat

3.1.1 Site and Context

Shahpur Jat Village is an urban village in South Delhi, located near Hauz Khas, within the remnants of the Siri Fort ruins. Literally translated it means "Royal Town of the Jats."

Figure 6
"Fashion Street" in
Shahpur Jat

The narrow, cramped lanes are dotted with traditional havelis and trendy fashion boutiques. At present, the demographics of Shahpur Jat Village mainly comprise Panwar Gotra Jats, who belong to a place in Ujjain, Madhya Pradesh, known as Dhara Nagri.[9] (Figure 3, page 17)

The village, which was initially known for its agricultural character is now shifting toward commercialization. This arose due to its proximity to affordable rentals and workshops from which supplies can be bought. The village is thriving thanks to handicrafts, weaving, craftwork, creative outputs, and the presence of many skilled craftspeople. In terms of the space's building typology, it has managed to create an extensive hybrid between the traditional heritage image of Delhi and the modern era. Due to this sudden shift in occupation, the population began to increase, and four- to five-story buildings started to emerge to accommodate it, replacing the once open public spaces, giving rise to increased volume and mass-sandwiching dark, narrow gullies (Figure 4, page 18). An interesting factor in this urban village is the segregation of the streets based on occupation and status, creating unofficial street names like "Village Street" and "Posh Street".

3.1.2 The Social Effect of Street Art in Shahpur Jat

St+Art India Foundation (St+Art) is a non-profit organization that aims to make streets more interactive through the medium of urban street art festivals across India. Artists from all over the world are invited to express themselves on blank, empty walls and leave their mark on them. In the Shahpur Jat Project, St+Art aimed to provide better spaces and give the area a certain identity and character through the use of color.

Figure 7
"Underwater Monster"
painting by YANTR in
Shahpur Jat

Parameter	Findings and analysis
Location	· Street art on "Posh Street" is restricted to formal fill colors that are used for purely aesthetic purposes to suggest the function of the space and is blended into the existing typology of the street. · In contrast, the rural streets have artwork in every nook and cranny. · There has been an informal growth of spaces with major artworks into active public nodes, which resulted from these artworks encouraging activities and people interactions in these spaces. · Land value around well-known street art started increasing as more people started buying areas and buildings near these places.
Physical attributes—color, scale, design	· On "Posh Street," color is used to identify the function of the space, with one solid color being used for each type of space. This color coding allows outsiders to gain a better understanding of the urban settlement. · In terms of scale, it can be seen that the larger the painting, the greater the impact it has on the space. Large paintings, such as "Cat Painting" and "Underwater Monster" have become markers in the space, while smaller paintings, although appreciated, do not have a large-scale impact. Over time, the streets began to be referred to by the artwork rather than the actual name of the street, thus shifting the identity of the space. · More simply designed street art, such as "Cat Painting," is more easily appreciated and accepted by the audience than complicated artworks such as "Underwater Monster," which tend to create more confusion. · We can infer that the paintings not only give the spaces an identity, but also, in the process, give them value and importance in the market. Through street art, the village has gained a certain identity that has helped increase its value and, hence, give it importance, which in turn has increased the value of the land.
User activity	· Streets with more artwork or large-scale artwork are bustling with activity and comparatively cleaner, due to the increase in user activity as the city makes more effort to maintain the area. · The impact created is more noticeable to tourists and outsiders than to locals.
Conception	· As many streets began to be referred to by their artwork, the conception of the space slowly started shifting to a new identity defined by the artwork.

Table 1
Data analysis and findings
for Shahpur Jat

"Shahpur Jat provided us with a very interesting space for an art intervention since we wanted to work in a high-density area that was also navigable by foot. Moreover, it is an urban village that was rapidly changing," said Akshat Nauriyal, content director at St+Art , in an interview with Suneet Zishan Langar for *ArchDaily*. He went on to explain that they started this project in 2014 with the dual intention of making public spaces more vibrant and interactive for the people who use them the most, and making art more democratic as a medium.

Through this, the importance of location and the role it plays in street art can be understood. Rapidly changing spaces or busy, crowded places are usually chosen to increase audience size and allow the art piece to interact with a broader audience. One of the co-founders of St+Art, Thanish Thomas, in an interview, spoke about the problems and complications St+Art needed to tackle when seeking permission for projects in Shahpur Jat. He elaborated on how residents were reluctant to allow the use of their walls and needed to be persuaded to do so. "Cat Painting," a popular local painting by street artist Anpu Varkey, known by the locals in Hindi as "Billi Walla" was key in getting people's agreement. Before "Cat Painting" was completed, gaining permission for street art was tedious, as few people were aware of exactly what street art was, and people were cautious about it. Over the years, this painting has become something of a landmark that people began referring to when identifying location or giving street directions. Thomas noted, "After the painting was done, people started calling the street the Billi Walla street." The painting gave the street a certain character that revolved around the painting, shifting the identity of the space (Figure 5, page 18).

Thomas explained how painting on the streets soon became more of an exchange program, where the artists would agree to paint what the locals wanted, or use their stories to get permission to use their walls. Through this exchange, the streets began to narrate the villagers' stories and transmit their culture and background through street art. The artists began to use this opportunity to paint the village's story and highlight its culture; instead of disrupting and ruining the existing character of the space, street art added to it and gave it a certain language that can be seen on the streets of Shahpur Jat.

Each painting has its own unique character, with an identity established by the artist, but which still follows a similar language, as the paintings narrate the story of the villagers and emphasize the village's culture. This adds to the village's heritage, rather than destroys it. It highlights the importance of the role of cultural and historical background in street art. Another of this group's initiatives was to paint the first floor of each street based on its function, which helps distinguish one space from another, in terms of functionality (almost like color-coding). This helped in the mapping of the village and created a uniform character for the streets. One striking example is the use of orange to indicate "Fashion Street." This is helpful in guiding tourists and other newcomers to the city and also gives the streets a certain character and direction in terms of design (Figure 6, page 20).

Another well-known painting that can be seen on the walls of Shahpur Jat is a mural by YANTR (*yantr* is Sanskrit for "machine"), a pseudonymous graffiti artist from Delhi whose vision is to make socio-political issues accessible to the general public through the medium of street art. His work revolves around the complexity of machines and organic forms, mixed together in his signature eclectic style.[10]

21

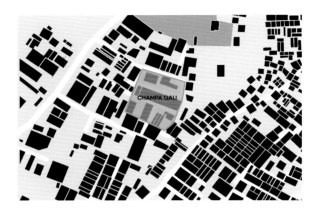

Figure 8
Plan view of Champa Gali

One of his paintings can be seen in Shahpur Jat and is commonly known by locals as "Underwater Monster." The painting is located along a residential area at the edge of the site along an informal small street and is now currently a major landmark of the area. What makes this painting famous is its use of bright colors and mechanical structures, which is an iconic trademark of most of YANTR's work. A unique feature of this painting is the addition of feathers to counterbalance the rigidity of this underwater jet, which gives the effect of sturdy weightlessness. In an interview with St+Art Festival, YANTR revealed that most of the locals were fascinated by the work, even as it was being painted. Back then, due to the complexity of the painting, it was referred to as "Tattoo Painting" by many people. With this "nickname," slowly, over time, even the identity of the space started to shift, as more activities started taking place near the painting, inadvertently creating a main public node. This led to a change in the character of the space and people began to refer to that small, informal street as "Tattoo Street," referring more to the painting than the actual function of the space/street. The painting is massive and covers an entire four-story-high wall. In terms of color, it is vivid, using bright colors to catch the audience's attention. From the "Cat Painting" and "Tattoo Painting" examples, we can see that each street has come to be referred to by the painting on it, hence changing the identity of the space (Figure 7, page 20).

After the completion of the project in Shahpur Jat, there was a certain shift in the character of the space. A wide range of audiences came to visit and admire the art on the walls. There was also a sudden shift in audience type. Due to this, an effort was made to retain the character of the space and keep it clean and presentable. No vehicles were allowed to enter the space. It was

Figure 9
A section of the main entrance street of Champa Gali

Figure 10
The Lioness in Champa Gali

consistently cleaned twice a day, and parking spaces were well controlled and organized.

A certain formal growth and development arose from this initiative, which gave rise to an ordered pattern. Large open spaces near such major artworks slowly started to become busy as more activities emerged around them, making these spots major activity nodes. When a local vendor was asked whether a painting right next to his shop had brought any changes, he replied, "People know the street by this painting now. I can hardly remember the time when it was not there. After it was completed, more people started buying land and building multistory buildings. Ever since these paintings, people have known about Shahpur Jat."

3.1.3 Data Analysis and Findings
The findings of the data collected on Shahpur Jat, and the corresponding analysis are summarized and listed in Table 1 (page 21).

3.2 Champa Gali

3.2.1 Site and Context
Champa Gali is a small street that grew amid Saidulajab Village in South Delhi. The street, known for its Parisian- and French-style boutique cafés, design studios, and handicraft shops, is a retail and commercial street that has recently gained prominence due to the "artsy" character of the space. Champa Gali, as such, was an unplanned project that grew unconsciously without any certain system or order to it. Its small, narrow streets are filled with cafés and street art, and open onto small squares that are all interconnected with one another, allowing the locals to be well connected with the various activities going on in the place (Figure 8, page 22).

According to a local shop owner, each café's artwork is designed by its owner and usually reflects the theme of the café. Funnily enough, there is a certain level of unity between each café's character that has, interestingly, come about unconsciously. The paintings and murals that can be seen along the walls are usually designed by the owners and painted by local artisans. Street art here is used by the locals as a form of advertisement and to attract tourists, as the majority of the locals are retail owners and there are hardly any residents. In terms of building typology, most of the buildings serve a purely retail function, and the massing is such that it allows for comparatively wide streets with more open spaces that blend in with the building massing. Moreover, the spaces do not contain high-story buildings; the buildings usually do not exceed two, or a maximum of three stories. This, along with the open spaces, gives the space a certain fluid character. Hence, the space is comparatively more open, creating more interactive spaces that allow natural light to enter. The area is comparatively small, and due to the smaller number of people, it allows for more community involvement (Figure 9, page 22).

3.2.2 Social Effect of Street Art in Champa Gali
Street art in Champa Village is mostly created by two local street artists, Gokul and Akshat. Akshat is a street artist or space maker with a background in industrial design and virtual reality, who believes in bringing art back to society. As a designer, he loves challenges and mainly aims to work on massive-scale works rather than works confined to canvas, that are restricted by the boundary of space: "I feel more connected with large-scale artworks,

Parameter	Findings and analysis
Location	· It is not connected to the cultural or historical background. Street art here is used mainly to attract more tourists and people to the space, and is aligned with the theme of the retail shops. · The location of the artwork directs people's movement patterns. For example, the painting *The Lioness* near the Social Street café directs most of the tourists toward the café, thus creating a larger crowd.
Physical attributes—color, scale, design	· Bright, contrasting colors are used to attract a larger audience and change the character of the space by making it bright and vibrant. The effect would not have been the same had the colors been dull and dark instead. · The scale of the paintings plays a major role in this context. The painting *The Lioness* is two stories high, occupying the entire entrance to the café, thereby making it a marker in the space. · The designs of most of the paintings follow a theme connected to the people and an overall theme in terms of design can be seen in the artworks present here, giving the entire space a unified character.
User activity	· Spaces with street art tend to create nodes for public gatherings and activities. They also divert people toward a space based on the location of the artwork, such as the painting *The Lioness*, which diverts people toward the café. This creates a shift in the hierarchy of spaces, making not only the painting, but also the open space around it a marker of space.
Conception	· This shift in both the direction of movement and the character of the space caused by street art creates a change in the way people interact with the space, thereby shifting its identity.

Table 2
Data analysis and findings
for Champa Gali

whereby the audience is not restricted. I like seeing people's different reactions when they walk by my art pieces."

His painting *The Lioness*, one of his early works, still stands as one of the major paintings with which Champa Gali is identified. The painting is a combination of a lion and a woman (Figure 10, page 23). When asked about the theme and idea behind the painting, he replied that a lioness has the will of a dragon and the beauty of a rainbow. He believes that his art can bring about a change in society and in people's mindsets, and their understanding of art: "You need to design spaces such that when you enter, (you consider) what is the first thing you see? You should be able to catch the eye and attention of your audience. Hence, more than painting, I'm also designing a user experience for every customer."

The painting is designed with the lioness facing the Social Street café, giving the arbitrary space a certain sense of directionality by "pulling" the crowd and guiding it on toward the café. This, helped the café gain more customers. According to Akshat, when a person enters Champa Gali, the first thing they notice is the painting; that is why the painting was made to face the Social Street café, and by way of that, helps increase its number of customers. On looking at the painting, people are immediately drawn by its color and scale, and tend to move automatically toward the café. The café uses this strategy to increase the number of customers it attracts.

Saket, the owner of the café next to *The Lioness* painting, revealed that the painting attracts many customers to his café and has helped increase his business. It has also created a great deal of variety in the crowd. People from various groups who were never part of the initial crowd at Champa Gali have come to visit the space and admire the artwork.

According to Saket, many fashion photographers and filmmakers have set up photoshoots by the painting.

Another major factor that must be taken into consideration is the painting's scale and bright, vivid colors, which effortlessly catches the eye of anyone who enters the town, arousing their curiosity. With its extravagant use of colors and massive scale, the painting exerts such dominance that tourists tend to refer to the area around the painting as the main central space, although geographically speaking, it is not so. This illustrates that street art can be used to shift public nodes and restructure spaces by changing the way people interact with them.

The shop Rekha and Renu is owned by and named after two sisters who are professional artists and who sell handmade crafts and paintings for a living. When asked if the cleanliness and maintenance of the space had changed at all due to these paintings, they replied, "Yes, a lot of effort is made to maintain it the way it is, and people are a lot more aware of the space and have a desire to keep it clean, which was not there before." They also explained how it has helped to attract more people and hence increase sales: "Many more tourists come to visit the area for its 'artsy' character and its huge wall paintings. This has increased the number of customers I receive and has helped me a lot."

We can infer that in Champa Gali, street art was originally intended simply to attract more customers; however, in the process of doing so, it created a conversation between the audience and the streets and led to an informal growth of various active nodes that were aligned in the direction of these artworks. Small active nodes slowly started to emerge where major artworks had been created. Street art is used here as a landscaping element to change the character of the space and bring more life to the place.

3.2.3 Data Analysis and Findings

The findings of the data collected on Champa Gali, and the corresponding analysis are summarized and listed in Table 2 (page 24).

4. Comparative Data Analysis and Findings

It should be noted that the main difference between these two case studies is the type of user group that interacts with the space. Shahpur Jat contains a mixed-user group that included retailers, residents, and others, whereas Champa Gali is a purely commercial space with only retail users. Another difference is in community involvement. In Shahpur Jat, an external organization brought about the change, however, in the case of Champa Gali, it was the locals who took the initiative to paint the walls, hence common process and administrative issues, such as needing permission and dealing with unease among locals were not factors that needed to be considered.

Other than the parameters discussed earlier, time is another factor that should be taken into consideration. In Champa Gali, most of the paintings were completed quite recently around 2019 and have just started to gain popularity among people, attracting various tourists and customers to the area. As the paintings are an installation that was only added recently, the change that has followed has not been drastic, but due to the difference in user groups, the process of its completion has been different and comparatively easier. Here, the change can be seen on a micro level and is noticeable, but has not, however, reached the macro level yet. In the case of Shahpur Jat, the paintings were completed much earlier around 2014, and a change has been brought about on a macro level, but is no longer noticeable on a micro level as time passed. We can, therefore, infer that as time passes, the effect produced in a certain space on a micro level diminishes, but it starts to gain a drastic and permanent identity shift on a macro level.

Some paintings have a lasting effect in an intangible sense by becoming markers of a space—which, as our study shows, is purely the result of the use of scale, color, location, and user activity—bringing about a change in the way each person pereceives the space. This slowly starts to change the character of the space, giving it a new identity.

5. Conclusion

The main objective an artist aims for is to leave their mark in time and create an identity through their work. Street art is used as a medium to narrate people's untold stories and to give the space a certain language. On a larger scale, it can be seen that street art can be used as a platform to revive once dead spaces and bring them back to use.

On a macro level, it can be seen that street art has gained in popularity and creates a sense of identity among the larger crowd, shifting the space's identity through the art, without losing the actual culture of the space. However, this was only achieved by incorporating the culture within the paintings. If done differently, the result would not have been like this, highlighting through this, the importance of the context in which each painting is made. The theme of most paintings usually revolves around the context in which they are situated, with a perfect blend of the artist's style incorporated into the art piece.

A "by-product" is how it can be used as a way of keeping a space clean. This is done by increasing the number of activities that happen on the street by creating a change in the physicality of the space through art, which indirectly affects the social activities that engulf that space, as Canter highlights. This increase in activity leads to an increase in interaction with the space and results in an urge to maintain the space with a certain decorum, thereby bringing about better living spaces, in terms of their physical appearance. The colors used have an impact on each person mentally and bring about a shift in the identity of the space. Although the artwork does make a mark on a macro level, the impact it has on a micro level is not the same.

On a micro level, among the locals, the effect that street art has, as of now, has its limits. Other than being a painting on the wall, it does not directly affect the locals unless they are stationed along the vicinity of the artwork or have an indirect connection to it. It creates thought and awareness among the people, but it does not bring about any tangible changes. This also depends upon the type of locals inhabiting the space and interacting with the piece, as seen in both case studies.

We conclude that each parameter, along with time, plays a massive role in the way art changes a space and shifts its identity and character. Street art can initially start to create small changes on a micro level, which can then slowly develop into a shift in identity on a macro level by creating a marker in the space.

Notes

1. Kristina Marie Gleaton, *Power to the People: Street Art as an Agency for Change* (Minnesota: University of Minnesota Digital Conservancy, 2019), 10.
2. Raymond Salvatore Harmon, *Bomb: A Manifesto of Art Terrorism* (United States: Creative Media Partners, LLC, 2018), 2–3.
3. S. Khoshkholghi, *Public Art: Livable Urban Public Spaces* (UK: AESOP-Young Academics Network, 2011), 2.
4. Kevin Lynch, *The Image of the City* (Cambridge, MA: MIT Press, 1960), 50–51.
5. David V. Canter, *The Psychology of Place* (London: Architectural Press, 1977), 158–160.
6. ibid.
7. "Let's Colour Social Experiments," letscolourproject, September 21, 2017, https://letscolourproject.com/surprising-paint-stories/lets-colour-social-experiments.
8. Patina Lee, "Changing the Urban Landscape in Rio Just Before the Olympics – JR is Our Artist of the Week Again!" *Widewalls*, August 4, 2016, https://www.widewalls.ch/magazine/jr-artist-of-the-week-august.
9. "Shahpur Jat Village, Delhi," Utsavpedia, August 10, 2013, https://www.utsavpedia.com/ethnic-hubs/delhis-fashion-hub-shahpur-jat-village.
10 "Indian Street Art Series," Swaraj Art Archive, July 21, 2015, https://swarajarchive.org.in/tag/yantr-graffiti.

Figure Credits

Figure 1: Bubble diagram (based on David Canter, *The Psychology of Place*, 1977) (authors' photo).
Figure 2: The self-fulfilling prophecy of place/activities (based on David Canter, *The Psychology of Place*, 1977) (authors' photo).
Figure 3: Plan view of Shahpur Jat, Delhi, 2019 (author's drawing).
Figure 4: Street section sketches of Shahpur Jat, Delhi, 2019 (authors' photos).
Figure 5: The famous "Cat Painting" by Anpu Varkey in Shahpur Jat, Delhi, 2015 (photographed by Akshat Naurial).
Figure 6: "Fashion Street" in Shahpur Jat, Delhi, 2016 (St+Art India Foundation, https://www.dfordelhi.in/7-food-outlets-shahpur-jat-cant-miss/).
Figure 7: "Underwater Monster" painting by YANTR in Shahpur Jat, Delhi, 2015 (photographed by Prakriti Gupta).
Figure 8: Plan view of Champa Gali, Delhi, 2019 (author's drawing).
Figure 9: A section of the main entrance street of Champa Gali, Delhi, 2019 (authors' photo).
Figure 10: *The Lioness* painting in Champa Gali, Delhi, 2019 (authors' photo).

An Investigation of Youth Homelessness and the Principles of Transitional Space Design

ZHOU Kai, The University of Melbourne, Australia
Greg MISSINGHAM*, The University of Melbourne, Australia

Abstract

Youth homelessness has become a global issue, with current figures estimated at 30 million young people worldwide, and projected to increase to 600 million by 2050. Typically, architects tackle this issue by either providing temporary shelter or building permanent housing. As such, more than just accommodation is needed. This paper uses Australia as the starting point for identifying the principles of transitional space design by redefining how a shelter functions, and by considering how humanizing spatial design characteristics could create a more holistic solution. The "collecting-- translating-- variance" framework was employed to collect quantitative and qualitative data and gain a deeper understanding of the current response to the youth homelessness crisis, as well as the experiences, journeys, and needs of homeless youths. The research revealed that the key to dealing with the homelessness crisis is in providing a comprehensive service structure—which, combines living spaces, rehabilitation spaces, education spaces, and sharing spaces. Aligned with the proposed principles, a transitional space would be a place where homeless youths are provided with quality permanent housing and where they can acquire practical occupational skills. This would enable young homeless people to reintegrate into society more quickly, and make a positive impression on the public. More broadly, by comparing the culture and policy in Australia with that of China, this study investigates whether these design principles can be used as a prototype in other countries and respond to each specific context.

Author Information
ZHOU Kai: herochowkay@outlook.com
Greg MISSINGHAM [*corresponding author]: G.missingham@unimelb.edu.au

Keywords

Youth homelessness, mental illness, humanizing space, design principles.

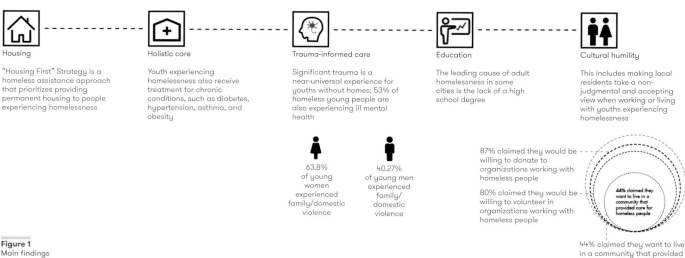

Housing
"Housing First" Strategy is a homeless assistance approach that prioritizes providing permanent housing to people experiencing homelessness

Holistic care
Youth experiencing homelessness also receive treatment for chronic conditions, such as diabetes, hypertension, asthma, and obesity

Trauma-informed care
Significant trauma is a near-universal experience for youths without homes; 53% of homeless young people are also experiencing ill mental health

Education
The leading cause of adult homelessness in some cities is the lack of a high school degree

Cultural humility
This includes making local residents take a non-judgmental and accepting view when working or living with youths experiencing homelessness

63.8% of young women experienced family/domestic violence

40.27% of young men experienced family/domestic violence

87% claimed they would be willing to donate to organizations working with homeless people

80% claimed they would be willing to volunteer in organizations working with homeless people

44% claimed they want to live in a community that provided care for homeless people

44% claimed they want to live in a community that provided care for homeless people

Figure 1
Main findings

1. Introduction

When discussing homeless youths, people tend to express animosity toward them and reflect the impression "they chose this lifestyle." However, as author Jeff Karabanow states, the belief that becoming homeless is a "choice" is inaccurate.[1]

Due to the impermanent nature of homelessness, the varying definitions of youth homelessness, and forms of hidden homelessness such as couch-surfing and doubling-up, it is hard to calculate an accurate total of homeless youth. Although existing figures are likely to underestimate the count of the homeless youth population, recent data indicates significant issues:
- The Australian Bureau of Statistics (ABS) reports that in 2016, young people aged 15–24 comprised 21 percent (around 24,200 young people) of the homeless population.[2]
- Centrepoint, a housing provider for young people reports that in 2019, in the United Kingdom, 121,000 young people aged 16–24 years old were homeless or at risk of being homeless.[3]
- The National Conference of State Legislatures (NCSL) reports that in 2019, in the United States, 4.2 million young people aged 13–25 years old were homeless or risk of being homeless.[4]

Because the definition of homelessness varies across different organizations and within different countries, in this paper, homeless youth are defined as those aged 15–24 years old, and living in one of the following situations:[5]
- With no shelter;
- In a place with no security of tenure;
- In a space with no control over the environment;
- In an inadequate dwelling that has no space to socialize; and
- Temporarily in other households (for example, with a friend or extended family member).

The path leading to homelessness is not usually one single, isolated event; the most common reasons for experiencing homelessness include housing crisis, domestic and family violence, and relationship or family breakdown. Additionally, homelessness has a dramatic influence on the lives of young people. If they are homeless, they are also more likely to disengage from education and employment.[6] Moreover, young people face many adverse consequences, such as developmental delays, and are at an increased risk of mental health problems or future trauma.[7] One study found that 42 percent homeless youth in Australia experienced mental health problems when they first became homeless, and this rate subsequently increases to 70 percent as they go down that road.[8] Additionally, those who experience homelessness at a young age are more likely to experience persistent homelessness during adulthood. Fortunately, younger people are more likely to escape persistent homelessness if appropriate interventions prevent them from becoming involved with drug use, unsafe sexual encounters, and violence.[9]

Although the youth homelessness crisis cannot be solved by architecture alone, architects who are unwilling to design spaces to manage this crisis, in turn, actually fail to interact with cities and their residents' needs. By implementing the "collecting (collecting data of homelessness)–translating (translating programs into architecture language)–variance" framework, this study investigates the current youth homelessness situation and analyzes young people's experiences, to explore how architecture can address this issue. The study proposes principles of transitional space design that provide homeless youths with quality permanent housing, and the practical occupational skills required to reintegrate into society quickly, while making a positive impression on the public. More broadly, by comparing Australia's culture and policy with China's, this study also tests whether these principles can be used as a prototype to be replicated in other countries and respond to each specific context.

2. Methodology

This study adopted the "collecting–translating–variance" framework to collect quantitative and qualitative data to gain a deeper understanding of the current response to the youth homelessness crisis and the experiences, journeys, and needs of homeless youths.

2.1 Collecting Data of Youth Homelessness
During the desk research portion—usually conducted during the initial phase of a study—data was collected from existing sources; preliminary research focused on homelessness statistics in Australia, and current homelessness services provided by the local government and charities to determine which programs are socially supported and community-oriented.

Spatial analysis focused on analyzing spatial design and architectural space intensity was also conducted. In recent decades, homelessness has created great concern in the architectural community. To understand how architecture can solve this problem, an analysis of current solutions proposed by supportive architects is required.

Currently, the primary solution to aid homelessness services is to provide temporary shelter, such as emergency shelters, tiny housing, or affordable housing, detailed as follows:
• Emergency shelters: emergency shelters are places where the homeless have a safe place to stay for a few nights.
• "Parasitic" housing: "parasitic" architecture involves construction that latches onto existing structures.
• Tiny houses: tiny houses are a permanent response to homelessness, such as building several tiny homes in a shared space.

2.2 Translating Programs into Architectural Languages
The next step was to identify activities and programs that cater to the needs of homeless youths to bring a positive change through flexible community activity, as what these youths need is more than just accommodation. The key to this part was in translating programs into architectural language to formulate function-based principles in transitional space design, while also facilitating positive change for young homeless people and wider society.

2.3 Variance
Youth homelessness exists in all countries and has become a global issue. This study, while responding to each country's unique context, more broadly, also investigates whether the prototype design principles proposed can be replicated in other countries.

This study also explores youth homelessness in China. By comparing Western countries' cultures and policies with China's, similar and different needs can be identified, and programs specific to China can be developed in response to its specific context.

3. Findings

To have a deeper understanding of the current response to the youth homelessness crisis, and the experiences, journeys, and needs of homeless youths, quantitative and qualitative data for Australia was collected through desk-based research, the spatial analysis of related projects, and observation. The main findings can be divided into five categories: housing, holistic care, trauma-informed care, education, and cultural humility (Figure 1, page 27).

3.1 Housing
On any given night in Australia, 26 percent of young people sleep on the streets, couch-surf, and seek shelter in unsafe accommodations.[10] The lack of suitable housing is the direct and primary cause of youth homelessness in Australia, which leads to these youths being exposed and thrust into harsh street life and the dangers within, as well as resulting in the disruption of education and stable and healthy social networks.[11]

Therefore, the priority of services engaging with homeless youths ensures their safety, wellbeing, and stability by providing housing. Currently, temporary shelters (Figure 2, page 29), such as emergency shelters and parasitic housing are the favored solutions to the youth homelessness crisis. However, this kind of accommodation is "sometimes so dilapidated, violent, and dirty, that people prefer to sleep outside."[12]

3.2 Holistic Care
Once young people have experienced homelessness, they face a growing risk of health problems and require treatments not only for common ailments like the cold, flu, and skin infections, but also for chronic conditions, such as diabetes, hypertension, asthma, and obesity. However, they tend to pay little attention to their health problems since they have competing priorities, and health needs are not at the top of their list unless an emergency occurs. In addition, they have limited access to primary care and medical treatment due to stigmatization.[13]

3.3 Trauma-informed Care
Many young people have become homeless also because of traumatic experiences of violence and abuse during childhood. A study conducted by Frontyard Youth Services, a specialist youth services provider to combat youth homelessness found that 63.8 percent of homeless young women and 40.27 percent of homeless young men had experienced family or domestic violence,[14] which indicates that family or domestic violence is the most common experience among most homeless youths.

Experiencing homelessness has a negative effect on young people's feelings, including making them feel useless, worthless, and abandoned. This results in poor mental health, like anxiety, depression, and fear. And if exposed to crime, violence, or exploitation, a young person's mental health can worsen, leading to using drugs to self-medicate. Based on this, traumatic experiences of domestic violence are both a cause and an effect of homelessness.[15]

3.4 Education
Homeless youths are also more likely to disengage from education and employment.[16] However, sometimes, the school can be a buffer for some young people suffering hardship, conflict, and instability at home as it can potentially be an agent/site for early intervention and engagement through targeted programs that create awareness and reach out in the process, reducing the risk of youth delinquency and substance abuse.[17] Without a high school certificate, homeless youths may experience limited access to

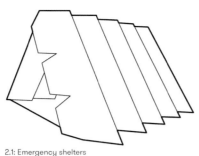

2.1: Emergency shelters

Cardboard Tents | Brussel

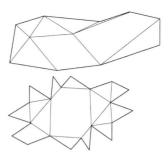

2.2: Emergency shelters

Cocoon
Hwang Kim

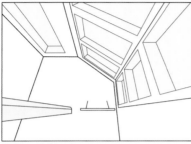

2.3: "Parasitic" housing

Homes for the homeless | London
Spatial Design Architects

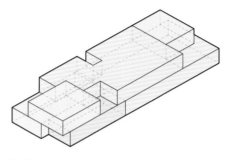

2.4: Housing

Shelter home for the homeless | Spain
Javier Larraz

Figure 2
Current response to the
youth homelessness crisis

employment opportunities, leading to financial hardships, housing instability, and eventually, homelessness in adult life.[18] As the education system improves and the job market changes, less than 9 percent of young people fail to graduate from high school, with many continuing to college. However, the high school dropout rate for homeless youths is 53 percent, with 51 percent currently not involved in education, employment, or training.

3.5 Cultural Humility

A survey conducted by Gallup, Inc., an American analytics company known for their worldwide public opinion polls found that 58 percent of people in the United States realize that homelessness is increasing nationwide, however, 49 percent believe that the number remains the same in their community,[19] which shows that people are reluctant to believe that the number of homeless people might be growing within their community.[20] In addition, there are many misconceptions, prejudices, and stereotypes about homeless youths. People express animosity toward these youth and have the impression that "they chose this lifestyle." On top of that, 56 percent claim that they would oppose living in a community that provided care for homeless people,[21] due to their fear of the homeless and their propensity for crime.[22]

The public's impression of homeless people can, sometimes, also be influenced by policies and services for the homeless within their towns and countries.[23] A negative impression of the homeless is associated with a lack of contact with the homeless.[24] On that aspect, one study found that people who joined such programs, like Youth Justice, or other homeless aid systems, have a higher possibility of participating in other programs.[25] This could mean that providing a space where homeless youths and the public can

communicate and share experiences could reduce the stigmatization of these youths by the community.

4. Principles of Transitional Housing Design

Based on the literature review and research findings on the current youth homelessness situation, it can be deduced that the key to managing the crisis is in identifying programs that meet the needs of homeless youths and facilitate positive change through flexible community programs. In architecture, the programs discussed in Section 3 are translated into creating two kinds of spaces—associated housing and community hubs consisting of rehabilitation space, education space, and sharing space. Each space is not innovative separately, but may facilitate positive changes when combined, to create an opportunity to eliminate the stigmatization of the homeless, as well as address the youth homelessness crisis.

4.1 Housing First: Associated Housing

Transitional space design will follow the "Housing First"[26] strategy, which as a first step, would provide young people experiencing homelessness with independent and permanent housing. It offers immediate access to permanent housing that is not contingent on readiness, or based on "compliance" (for example, sobriety). Instead, this is a rights-based intervention rooted in the idea that everyone is entitled to a home, and that adequate housing is a prerequisite for recovery.[27] The "Housing First" strategy affirms that access to stable housing is a fundamental right, and that homeless youths will do better and recover more efficiently once this need is satisfied. This strategy has proven successful in dealing with the youth homelessness crisis.

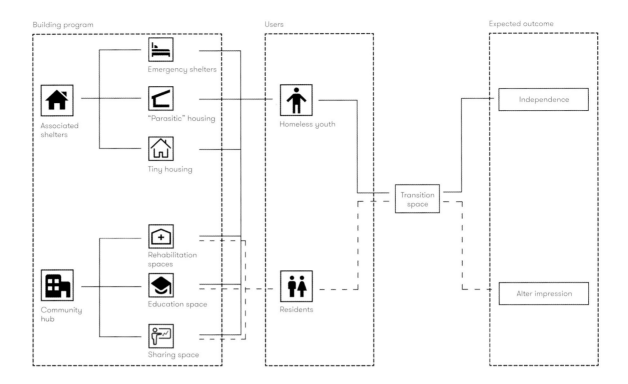

Figure 3
Programmatic solutions

Building program · Users · Expected outcome

Emergency shelters
Associated shelters
"Parasitic" housing
Tiny housing
Community hub
Rehabilitation spaces
Education space
Sharing space
Homeless youth
Residents
Transition space
Independence
Alter impression

4.2 Beyond Housing: The Community Hub

Earlier, it was highlighted that homeless youths need more than just accommodation to overcome homelessness. Though there is convincing evidence that the long-term experience of homelessness is detrimental to health and personal safety, in addition to being shocking and stressful for young people, it is surprising that there is sometimes reluctance among people to lend aid. Such negative responses toward homeless youths without providing them the support they need to help them get out of the situation can contribute to negative long-term consequences for young people.

A community hub that houses a rehabilitation space, education space, and shared space could help young people stay connected to their community and school, and strengthen their connections to natural sources of support to prevent and reduce the risk of long-term homelessness. Beyond that, it could also serve as a platform for the youths to share their experiences and for both homeless youth and public to communicate and share thoughts and experiences, which could alter people's perceptions of homeless young people. At the same time, it could provide an opportunity for these young homeless people to become valued members of society; for example, in a retail space, youths could learn direct occupational skills.

4.2.1 Rehabilitation Space

Considering that 53 percent of homeless young people are also experiencing ill mental health,[28] which is another factor that can be considered both a cause and effect of homelessness,[29] it is essential to provide programmatic spaces that respond to combating the leading causes of youth homelessness, to give access to proper care. This rehabilitation space should include:

- Counseling space: as mental health problems are both cause and effect of youth homelessness,[30] by providing a counseling space within areas where they live to address mental stress and issues, homeless youths can have access to proper care.
- Pharmacy/ health clinic: once they have experienced homelessness, young people face a growing risk of health problems that include common ailments (flu, cold, and skin infections) and chronic conditions (asthma, hypertension, and obesity). The provision of a pharmacy space will provide these young people access to primary care and medical treatment within the housing complex.
- Green space: considering research has shown that access to green spaces can improve one's mood and help treat mental health problems,[31] providing a green space should be an essential element of transitional space design.

4.2.2 Education Space

Young people may, over time, develop the necessary skills to live on the streets, but they may not have an opportunity to acquire the practical life skills that will allow them to be independent in the future. Education and practical skills are required to provide homeless young people with employment opportunities that can end the cycle of poverty. Although providing an education space is not a permanent solution, it provides a stepping-stone toward ending homelessness, since the leading cause of adult homelessness in some cities is the lack of a high school leaving certificate.[32] The education space will include:

- Classrooms: by providing classrooms for education, homeless young people will have a better chance to complete their high school education and gain a decent job to end the cycle of homelessness.

Name		Stock	Location	Scale	Basic Function	Layout
China	Yangzhou Welfare Centre	Government	Urban-rural fringe: Yangzhou	108	Housing, trauma-informed care	Closed
	Nanjing Relief Station	Government	Urban-rural fringe: Nanjing	550	Housing, protection center for minors	Closed, family-oriented
Western countries	Youth Projects, Australia	Charity	Urban area: Melbourne and other areas across Victoria	699	Housing, trauma-informed care, living skill	Semi-open, community-oriented
	Step Up, United States	Charity	Urban area: Los Angeles, Inland Empire, Orange County	1,000	Housing, living skill	Community-oriented
	Centrepoint, United Kingdom	Charity	Urban area: London, Manchester, Yorkshire	1,107	Housing, health support, living skill	Community-oriented

Table 1
A comparison of current transitional spaces in China with those in Western countries

- Maker space: in addition to formal education, trade-based skills training could provide an extra opportunity for young homeless people to acquire a job in the future.

4.2.3 Sharing Space

There are many misconceptions, prejudices, and stereotypes about youth homelessness, and the public's impression of homeless young people is often influenced by homelessness policies and services rendered to these youths;[33] sometimes, the negative impression also stems from a lack of contact with the homeless.[34] Therefore, a space for both youth and public to communicate and share their experiences could reduce the unfavorable stigmatization. In addition, a sharing space would provide an opportunity for homeless youths to learn direct occupational skills and become valued members of society through participation in community activities. The sharing space should include:

- Library: Research has found that only 44 percent of people are willing to live in a community that provides care for homeless people, given the stigma of homelessness and the prejudices against homeless youths. The library would be a space to acquire knowledge, as well as be a platform for both youth and public to have exchanges with each other to raise awareness of youth homelessness.
- Commercial space: a commercial space, including retail stores and restaurants, would provide homeless youths with opportunities to learn direct occupational skills and establish a life/work-based relationship, which will help create a sense of being a valued member of society.

To summarize, the physical space can affect a person's moods and behaviors,[35] and shelter makes a difference in how users see themselves and the world. By incorporating the design principles listed above, a transitional space will be a place where homeless youths can have quality permanent housing and acquire valuable occupational skills, and simultaneously, help the public form an accurate impression on youth homelessness (Figure 3, page 30).

However, there are, of course, also other considerations to include when designing a space for young homeless people. These are:
- Maintenance and durability—material maintenance and durability should also be considered when designing a facility for the homeless, especially for residents with mental health and substance abuse problems. At the same time, the environment must be comfortable so that residents in these facilities can sleep properly, and rest to recover from everyday stresses.
- Multi-use—homeless shelters often have multiple functions, including dining, showering, and laundry facilities, and other related amenities and programs. Therefore, designers need to consider the feasibility of spatial design and transformation.

5. Variance

Youth homelessness exists in all countries and has become a global issue. This study also investigated whether the ideas discussed can be used as a prototype to be replicated in other cities, and respond to each unique situation within individual contexts.

A comparison of the current transitional spaces in China with those in other Western countries (Table 1) revealed that Western countries pay more attention to breaking the cycle of homelessness, while the welfare centers in China focus on attending to basic living needs. Even then, it is worthwhile to highlight that the many young people experiencing homelessness face the same problems worldwide and have the same needs, hopes, and aspirations as other young people. Hence, the transitional space design principles listed above could also be applied in China. However, designers should pay more attention to the location of these transitional spaces to ensure they do not become a barrier to accessing the services that are provided, as most welfare centers in China, so far, are located in rural areas, where people do not have convenient public transport access. In addition, cultural appropriateness needs to be considered, particularly when it comes to minority groups.

6. Conclusion

This study focused on the youth homelessness crisis through the "collecting–translating–variance" method to collect quantitative and qualitative data, and it is determined that the best way to deal with the crisis is to identify programs that meet the needs of homeless youths, and facilitate positive change through flexible community involvement. Therefore, this study proposes that the following design principles should be used to construct transitional spaces for homeless youths: associated housing, plus a community hub—consisting of rehabilitation spaces, education spaces, and sharing spaces—to work together with other spaces to bring about a positive change in the lives of the youths. By incorporating the proposed principles, transitional spaces for homeless youths could offer quality permanent housing and support the acquisition of practical occupational skills. This will enable homeless youths to reintegrate into society smoothly with little repercussions, especially where public impression is concerned. Moreover, this study also explored the feasibility of replication in other cities, like China, and the results show that by refining some spatial elements, these principles could be applied in other cities and respond to each specific context.

Notes

1. Jeff Karabanow, "Becoming a Street Kid: Exploring the Stages of Street Life," *Journal of Human Behaviour in the Social Environment*, Vol. 13 (2006): 49–72.
2. Australian Bureau of Statistics, "Census of Population and Housing: Estimating, 2016," Canberra, 2016.
3. Centrepoint data, 2016, https://centrepoint.org.uk/databank/.
4. National Conference of State Legislatures (NCSL), "Youth Homelessness Overview 2019," https://www.ncsl.org/research/human-services/homeless-and-runaway-youth.aspx.
5. City of Melbourne, "What is Homelessness," (2016), https://www.melbourne.vic.gov.au/community/health-support-services/social-support/about-homelessness/Pages/about-homelessness.aspx.
6. Department of Families, Community Services and Indigenous Affairs, "Literature Review: Effective Interventions for Working with Young People Who are Homeless or at Risk of Homelessness" (2012), Canberra, Australia.
7. United States Interagency Council on Homelessness, "Homelessness in America: Focus on Youth," (2018), https://www.usich.gov/resources/uploads/asset_library/Homelessness_in_America_Youth.pdf.
8. Caludine Martijn and Louise Sharpe, "Pathways to Youth Homelessness," *Social Science and Medicine* 62, no. 1 (2006): 1–12.
9. Australian Bureau of Statistics, "Census of Population and Housing: Estimating, 2016."
10. ibid.
11. Jessica A. Heerde and George C. Patton, "The Vulnerability of Young Homeless People," *Lancet* 5, no. 6 (2020): E302–03.
12. "Why Some Homeless Choose the Streets Over Shelters," *NPR*, Talk of the Nation program, December 6, 2012, on-air interview and online transcript, https://www.npr.org/2012/12/06/166666265/why-some-homeless-choose-the-streets-over-shelters.
13. Andrew Davies and Lisa J. Wood, "Homeless Health Care: Meeting the Challenges of providing Primary Care," *Medical Journal of Australia* 209, no. 5 (2018): 230–234.
14. Frontyard Youth Services, "What is Youth Homelessness" (2018), Melbourne City Mission (mcm.org.au).
15. John Coates, J., and Suzie McKenzie-Mohr, "Out of the Frying Pan, Into the Fire: Trauma in the Lives of Homeless Youth Prior to and During Homelessness," *Journal of Sociology and Social Welfare* 37, no. 4 (2010): 65–96.

16. Department of Families, Community Services and Indigenous Affairs, "Literature Review: Effective Interventions for Working with Young People Who are Homeless or at Risk of Homelessness."
17. John Crank, Joe Crank, and Wendy Christensen, "The Ada Sheriffs Youth Foundation: The Development of a Decentralized Youth Program," *Journal of Criminal Justice* 31, no. 4 (2003): 341–350.
18. Brittany Sznajder-Murray et al., "Longitudinal Predictors of Homelessness: Findings from the National Longitudinal Survey of Youth – 97," *Journal of Youth Studies* 18, no. 8 (2015): 1,015–1,034.
19. Fannie Mae (for Gallup Inc.), "Homelessness in America: Americans Perceptions, Attitudes and Knowledge – General Population Survey and City Surveys" (2017).
20. ibid.
21. ibid.
22. Amy Melissa Donley, "The Perception of Homeless People: Important Factors in Determining Perceptions of the Homeless as Dangerous," University of Central Florida, electronic theses and dissertations, 2008.
23. Jack Tsai et al., "Changes in Public Attitudes and Perceptions about Homelessness Between 1990 and 2016," *American Journal of Community Psychology* 60, no. 3/4 (2017): 599–606, Wiley Online Library, https://onlinelibrary.wiley.com/doi/abs/10.1002/ajcp.12198.
24. Barrett A. Lee, Chad R. Farrell, and Bruce G. Link, "Revisiting the Contact Hypothesis: The Case of Public Exposure to Homelessness," *American Sociological Review* 69, no.1 (2004): 40–63.
25. AIHW (Australian Institute of Health and Welfare), "Children and Young People at Risk of Social Exclusion: Links Between Homelessness, Child protection and Juvenile Justice," data linkage series no. 13, cat. no. CSI 13, 2017, Canberra.
26. Wikipedia, https://de.wikipedia.org/wiki/Housing_First.
27. Stephen Gaetz and Bill O'Grady, "Why Don't You Just Get a Job? Homeless Youth, Social Exclusion, and Employment Training" in Stephen Gaetz et al., eds., *Youth Homelessness in Canada: Implications for Policy and Practice*, (Toronto: Canadian Observatory on Homelessness Press, 2013), 243–268.
28. Orygen, The National Centre of Excellence in Youth Mental Health, "Clinical Practice in Early Psychosis Working with Young People," 2016.
29. Coates and McKenzie-Mohr, "Out of the Frying Pan, Into the Fire."
30. ibid.
31. National Health Care for the Homeless Council, "Engaging Youth Experiencing Homelessness," Washington, 2016.
32. ibid.
33. Tsai et al., "Changes in Public Attitudes and Perceptions about Homelessness Between 1990 and 2016."
34. Lee, Farrell, and Link, "Revisiting the Contact Hypothesis: The Case of Public Exposure to Homelessness."
35. Jill Pable, "Shelter Design Can Help People Recover from Homelessness," *The Conversation*, July 5, 2018, https://theconversation.com/shelter-design-can-help-people-recover-from-homelessness-98374.

Figure Credits
Figure 1: Main findings (drawn by Zhou Kai).
Figure 2: Current response to the homelessness crisis.
    Figure 2.1 Cardboard Tents, Brussel ("Cardboard Tents Distributed to Brussels Homeless," *BBC News* December 29, 2017, https://www.bbc.com/news/world-europe-42517710?utm_medium=website&utm_source=archdaily.com).
    Figure 2.2 Cocoon, Hwang Kim, 2015 ("Hwang Kim: Urban Homeless Cocoon," *Designboom*, https://www.hwangkim.com/project_14.html#none).
    Figure 2.3 Homes for the Homeless, Spatial Design Architects, London (Eric Oh, "These Detachable Pods Aim to Provide Shelter for Britain's Homeless," Architecture News, *ArchDaily*, July 21, 2015, https://www.archdaily.com/770386/these-detachable-pods-aim-to-provide-shelter-for-britains-homeless).
    Figure 2.4 Shelter Home for the Homeless, Javier Larraz, Spain ("Shelter Home for the Homeless," "Projects–Houses–Spain" section, *ArchDaily*, April 5, 2011, https://www.archdaily.com/124688/shelter-home-for-the-homeless-javier-larraz?ad_source=search&ad_medium=search_result_all).
Figure 3: Programmatic solutions (drawn by Zhou Kai).

Kids Smile Labo Nursery

Various plants are placed along the steps in the nursery

Architect firm: Hibinosekkei, Youji no Shiro
Principal architect: Hibinosekkei, Kids Design Labo
Location: Atsugi, Kanagawa, Japan
Area: 340.08 square meters
Completion date: 2021
Photography: Hibinosekkei

This is a nursery on the second floor of a building in Atsugi, Kanagawa, designed and managed by architectural design office Hibinosekkei, which specializes in designing kindergartens and welfare facilities.

Many elements of the forests in Atsugi have been incorporated in the interior design to create a lively, child-friendly environment where children can be themselves, explore through imagination, and build confidence with play, exercise, and learning.

Trail steps—there are many steps in this nursery although it is a limited space, providing children with plenty of opportunities to move their limbs and benefit with exercise as they play.

Forest in a building—various plants are placed along the steps, so that children can still be in touch with greenery even when indoors. As the plants change with the seasons, and sprout and bloom, they can learn about their life cycle and observe live examples.

Cave atelier—the atelier is surrounded by low walls, as above, so that children can concentrate on drawing while being "blocked" from the adults' eyes, while simultaneously blocking out adults from their periphery. The inside wall is a blackboard surface that allows the children to have fun "drawing on the walls" with chalk. Some portions are also magnetized to display fun artworks or announcements.

Explorer library—next to the atelier is a bookshelf that displays an aquarium and some insect cages. Next to those are arranged picture books and encyclopedias about animal life, bugs, and creatures to encourage the children to look up a particular insect species and its behavior as they take the time to observe them. This helps to build their curiosity to learn and discover, and facilitates an independence to seek out information on their own.

Secret path—next to the explorer library is a narrow path that is lined with a shelf of toys for the play house. This space faces east and children can let their imagination glow like the warm sun rays that filter in. There is also a long planter in this space for growing vegetables and experiencing the feel of earth between the fingers as they garden and harvest vegetables.

View counter—at the top step, there is a counter where the children can enjoy the city

view. They can also use this space as a reading perch, burying their noses in one of the picture books from the shelf, or indulge in some me-time watching the world go by as they have their lunch on this perch.

Mirror pond—the restroom space is surrounded by mirrored walls. This imparts a sense of openness and continuity in the environment and helps the area feel less cramped, even though the restroom is located within the classroom. This mirror wall can be a place for children to draw, enjoy the amusement of reflections, or come up with creative ways to play.

Forest dining—the height of the kitchen counter is tailored to accommodate the children's low height and small size, so that they can prepare their own lunch, and through that, decide for themselves how much they should eat, what they should eat, and so on. The low counter also makes it easy for children to communicate with the chefs. This design aims to stimulate the children's interest in food and food preparation and aid toward building the ability and skill to prepare meals for themselves.

These design elements shape a model representation of a nursery in the building, as well as tailor an enriching space for the children, where they are nurtured, can discover themselves, learn at their pace, and blossom freely.

Cave atelier

The characteristic of KSL is long steps, which allow children to run around, instead of the enclosed classroom

The atelier can be seen from the top step

Secret path area facing east, where children can enjoy the sun rays beaming in

Cocooned within the low walls of cave atelier

Children can observe the scenes outside, such as the train moving, as they look out the long set of windows

Mirrored walls extend continuity within the space and open up the area

Drawing on the mirrored walls of the restroom

Explorer library

Books are displayed on the long bookshelf for children to easily pick out the ones they like

Tall plants and bushy shrubbery create the impression of a forest

Forest dining area

Reading at the view counter

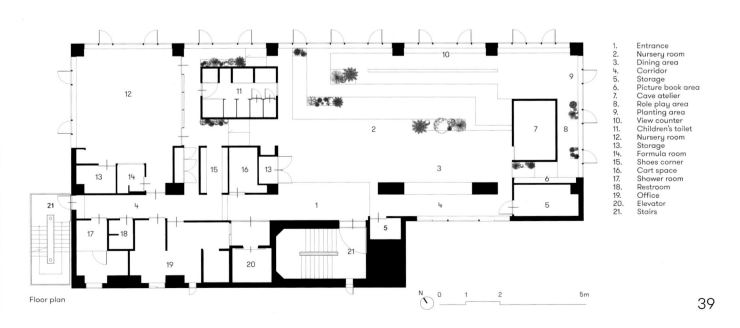

Floor plan

1. Entrance
2. Nursery room
3. Dining area
4. Corridor
5. Storage
6. Picture book area
7. Cave atelier
8. Role play area
9. Planting area
10. View counter
11. Children's toilet
12. Nursery room
13. Storage
14. Formula room
15. Shoes corner
16. Cart space
17. Shower room
18. Restroom
19. Office
20. Elevator
21. Stairs

N 0 1 2 5m

Sukagawa Community Center

External appearance

Architect firm: Ishimoto Architectural & Engineering Firm, Unemori Architects
Location: Sukagawa City, Fukushima Prefecture, Japan
Total floor area: 13,698 square meters
Completion date: August 2018
Photography: Kawasumi | Kobayashi Kenji Photograph Office

The Sukagawa Community Center in Fukushima is a part of a municipal reconstruction project to revitalize the severely damaged city center after the Great East Japan Earthquake in 2011. Following a series of citizen workshops, the architects developed a multipurpose building complex extending five floors. Built in collaboration with Ishimoto Architectural & Engineering Firm, the community center's architecture by Unemori Architects is characterized by open floor setbacks, cantilevered slabs, and an activity-based floor plan, transcending the building typology of a public community center, thereby, successfully connecting the city and its people.

Revitalizing the City Center

The community center aims to regenerate community life and revitalize the severely destroyed city center. By incorporating the public's request—

gathered through citizen workshops—in the design of the multipurpose community building, the Sukagawa Community Center is created as a public forum, connecting the city and its citizens.

The center includes a library, childcare services, and a three-dimensional play space, as well as a museum, a lecture hall, and a café, among other facilities and amenities. With a total floor area of 13,698 square meters, extending over five floors, the center offers various socializing spaces and rental rooms for studying, as well as several inner and outer terraces that surround the whole building.

A Complex Structural System

The center is designed as an interlocked structure based on different floor slabs, divided into small sections and staggered, to form an incremental setback on the site facing the historic main street. The building's architecture, thus, offers many terraces, providing further outdoor activity and socializing spaces, while the recessive façade of the building allows sufficient distance from the neighboring houses.

The interior structure is characterized by an open floor plan and offset floor levels that partly appear to float freely in the cavity of the center, creating various voids and dynamic open views throughout the different

floor slabs. In order to realize this complex structural system, a megastructure comprising the third and fourth floors—that entails a steel frame composed of trusses— was designed. The cantilevered slab of the lower floor is suspended from the megastructure and supported by columns on the upper floors, the positions of which are shifted accordingly to bear the load. Further, the trusses provide space for the installation of air-conditioning equipment, as well as smoke exhaust routes in case of a fire; it also serves as a sound-absorbing layer protecting the quiet environment of the library on the upper floors from noise filtering in from the lower floors. The upper floors are connected by gentle slopes and stairs, which allow visitors to walk around the entire building as if taking a walk around the city.

The first floor, which serves as the main entrance to the facility, is a sloping space integrating the 2.5-meter elevation difference of the site. The waiting area, café, and event space located on the first floor are connected with the outdoor space and seamlessly integrated into the hilly cityscape of Sukagawa. The second floor houses children-focused amenities, such as a kids' library and an open, two-story playground. Located on the third floor is the main library, as well as a number of rental rooms and inner terraces, which allow for

Aerial view

quiet working, and which also provide socializing spaces, respectively. The library extends across the fourth floor, where more rental rooms and an open community space are located. The museum is located on the fifth floor of the facility.

Connecting the City and its Citizens
The Sukagawa Community Center offers a wide range of cultural and recreational activities that are assigned different activity themes, such as "Raise," "Play," "Create," "Learn," and "Meet." The facility is divided into different areas of action offering various opportunities for people to meet, to engage in activities, and to interact with knowledge. The Sukagawa Community Center is designed to transcend functional boundaries and enable a complex experience by reinterpreting the building typology of a public community center. With the complex structural layout of the community center, as well as the reclassification from conventional categories into activity-oriented themes, an architectural solution that addresses the need for a public forum and which simultaneously creates a long-lasting and versatile relationship between the city and its citizens is provided.

View of the walkway

Entrance street

Entrance street

Entrance street

Main library

Main library

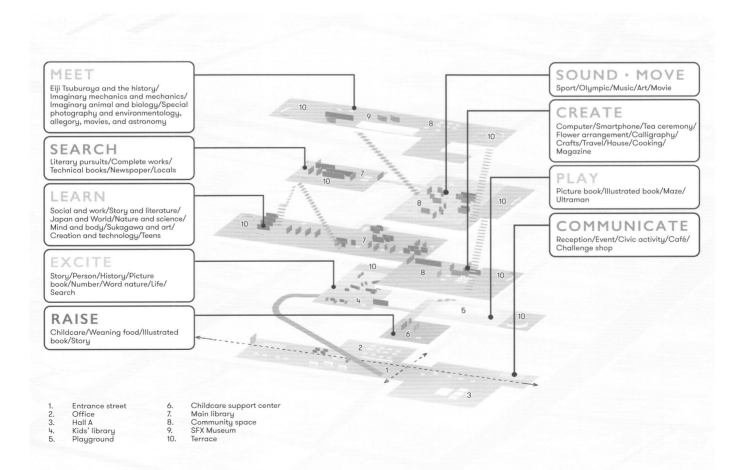

1. Entrance street
2. Office
3. Hall A
4. Kids' library
5. Playground
6. Childcare support center
7. Main library
8. Community space
9. SFX Museum
10. Terrace

MEET
Eiji Tsuburaya and the history/
Imaginary mechanics and mechanics/
Imaginary animal and biology/Special
photography and environmentology,
allegory, movies, and astronomy

SEARCH
Literary pursuits/Complete works/
Technical books/Newspaper/Locals

LEARN
Social and work/Story and literature/
Japan and World/Nature and science/
Mind and body/Sukagawa and art/
Creation and technology/Teens

EXCITE
Story/Person/History/Picture
book/Number/Word nature/Life/
Search

RAISE
Childcare/Weaning food/Illustrated
book/Story

SOUND · MOVE
Sport/Olympic/Music/Art/Movie

CREATE
Computer/Smartphone/Tea ceremony/
Flower arrangement/Calligraphy/
Crafts/Travel/House/Cooking/
Magazine

PLAY
Picture book/Illustrated book/Maze/
Ultraman

COMMUNICATE
Reception/Event/Civic activity/Café/
Challenge shop

Axonometric diagram

Main library

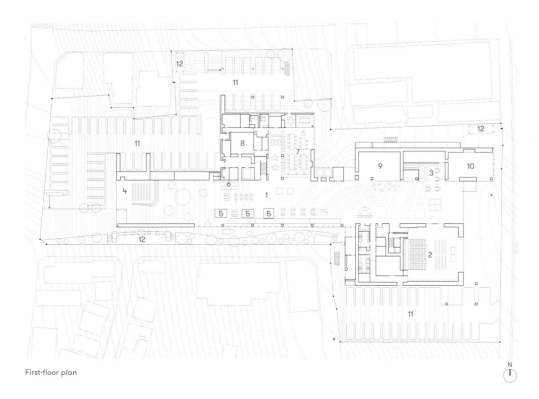

First-floor plan

1. Entrance street
2. Hall A
3. Civic activity support center
4. Hall B
5. Shop
6. Café
7. Office
8. Library office
9. Convenience store
10. Rental room
11. Parking
12. Bicycle parking
13. Kids' library
14. Playground
15. Childcare support center
16. Main library
17. Research library
18. Community space
19. FM studio
20. SFX Museum
21. Study room
22. Inner terrace
23. Terrace
24. Void

N

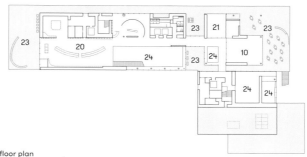

Fifth-floor plan

Fourth-floor plan

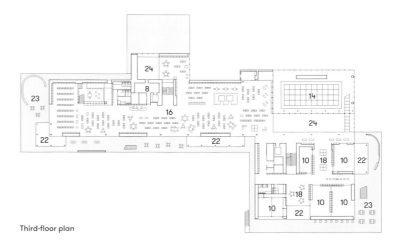

Third-floor plan

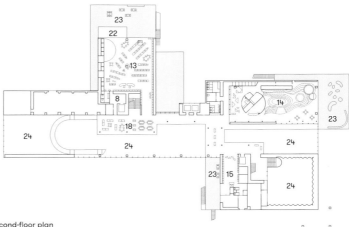

Second-floor plan

Kids' library

Inner terrace

Kids' park

Terrace

Inner terrace

1. Entrance street
2. Hall
3. Community space
4. Playground
5. Terrace
6. Inner terrace
7. Main library
8. Research library
9. Rental room
10. SFX Museum

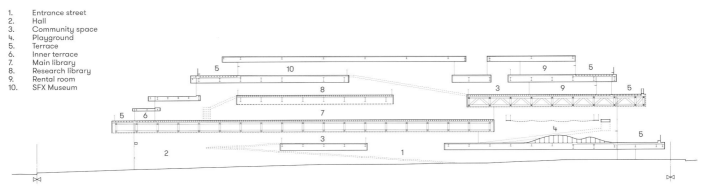

Section

St. Andrews Institute of Technology and Management: Boys' Hostel Block

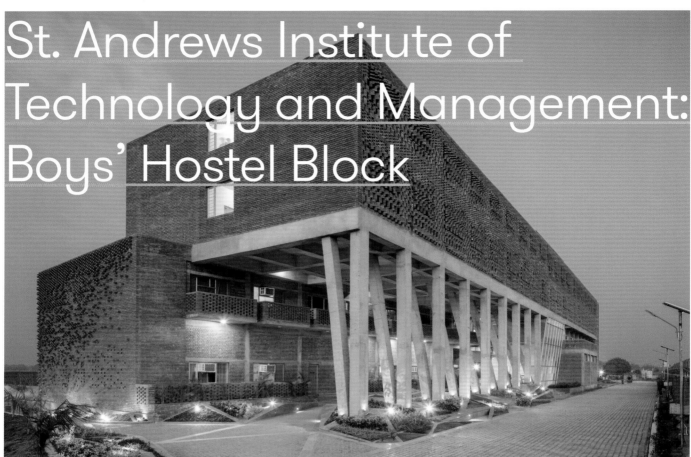

The brick envelope demonstrates innovation in sustainability

Architect firm: Zero Energy Design Lab (ZED Lab)
Principal architect: Sachin Rastogi and
Payal Rastogi
Design team: Rohan Mishra, Naveen Pahal,
Tanya Makker, Arya Kaushik
Location: Gurugram, India
Area: 5,574 square meters
Completion date: 2017
Photography: Noughts and Crosses | Andre
J. Fanthome

The boys' hostel block at St. Andrews Institute of Technology and Management is a meticulously designed, well-engineered residential complex that obtains its character from the basic building block—the brick. The building maintains a strong horizontal emphasis and utilizes a restrained material palette, consisting of exposed fair-faced concrete in the robust support structure of the façade. The design of the hostel block creates a sense of community and reflects the contemporary nature of the university buildings. It houses a fluid sequence of socially functional and environmentally sustainable spaces.

Planning and Design Strategies
The building reinterprets Indian vernacular architecture with ideas and techniques relevant to the present time. Anticipating the importance of student interaction with the spaces and the landscape around them, as well as the interactions between themselves, the galactic indoor spaces are design extensions of the exterior. The layered interior planning of the building, with passive design strategies, facilitates comfortable intercommunication among the students.

The contorted central atrium allows natural light to penetrate deeper into the building. It also acts as a solar chimney that takes away the stale and hot air within the building through a stack effect. The block accommodates residential units for 360 students, with recreational courts and mess facilities included. The triple-height spacious dorms depart from the conventional style of dorms, providing an enhanced user experience and a more expansive view of the outdoors to the students.

The combination of the angled volume of part of the ground floor and the linear shape of the first floor creates a shaded entrance (summer court) and an open terrace (winter court) on the south and north façades, respectively. The interactive composition forms the social heart of the block, creating a stimulating experiential space for students to engage

in discussions, socialize, or withdraw into for some alone time.

The landscaped ramp located within the summer court acts as a transition space between the harsh outdoors and the relaxed indoors, protecting students from thermal shock. This ramp leads to the light-filled cafeteria, which reinforces, on a large scale, the university's focus on generous spaces for students to interact in.

The serendipitous creation of the winter court on the first floor in the north direction enables one to enjoy the weather during summer evenings and winter afternoons. The terrace overlooks the playing field and establishes a visual dialogue with the overall context of the campus's greenery and other buildings.

Construction Methodology: Innovation
ZED Lab believes that sustainability is not separate from design, and design teams thrive on designing sustainable interventions as indispensable components that enhance the experience of the built environment. Therefore, factors such as the orientation of the building, materiality, and creation of spaces in the hostel block derive existence through comprehensive research based on climatic conditions, sun path analysis, and air movement.

Boys' hostel façade

Boys' hostel façade

The brick envelope of the building harnesses software technology, such as Ecotect, Grasshopper, Ladybird, and Rhino to create a sustainable design narrative. The use of software technology and computational studies is pertinent to the design of the brick *jaali* that circumscribes the building, providing thermal insulation and the ingress of diffused natural light. The simulations, or the parametric scripts, designed using software, and conclusions drawn from the analysis of climatic conditions, provide the existing radiation and the appropriate amount of radiation that should enter through the façade. By later running simulations on each brick, a composition is derived—comprising arrangements/layers of bricks rotated and then placed at regular intervals.

The *jaali* façade has 2.54-centimeter-thick steel bars fixed on RCC (reinforced cement concrete) beams using Hilti chemicals. To hold the brick arrangement, a single steel bar pierces through the customized bricks manufactured with holes; no cement mortar has been used to construct the 6.5-meter-long *jaali* envelope.

Presently, the *jaali* profile and its composition are essential factors that reduce the heat energy of direct radiation by 70 percent, thus providing comfortable, habitable spaces. However, the *jaali* also provides daylighting levels in the dorms equal to 250 lux. The balconies located within the brick skin are 1.2 meters wide. The balconies (or the buffer zones) between indoor and outdoor spaces control the mean temperature of the building throughout the year.

The composition of the 21-foot-long *jaali* façade reduces the heat energy of direct radiation by 70 percent

The 4-foot-wide balconies act as buffer zones between indoor and outdoor spaces

Stacking pattern

1. Regular stretcher bond
2. Staggered to allow natural daylight in
3. Stacking pattern to further improve filtering light
4. Rotated to enhance mutual shading

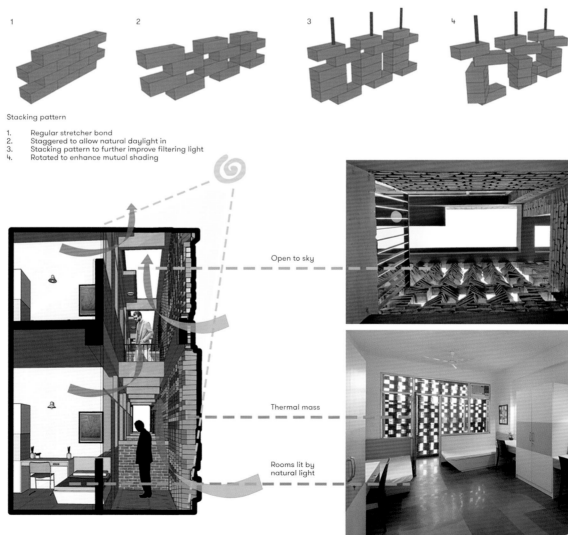

Open to sky

Thermal mass

Rooms lit by natural light

Boys' hostel analysis sheet

1. Landscape ramp
2. Foyer
3. Reception
4. Cafeteria
5. Kitchen
6. Gym
7. Room
8. Medical room
9. Laundry
10. Restrooms
11. Terrace
12. Dormitory
13. Recreation zone
14. Landscape seating
15. Sky-lit atrium

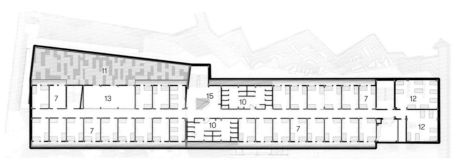

First-floor plan

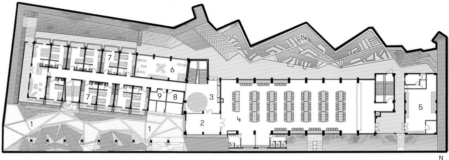

Ground-floor plan

N

Transition space

Interior area

Boys' hostel façade–view from inside

Brick jaali
(thermal mass)

Winter court
overlooking
playground

Summer
(81 °Fahrenheit)

Winter
(60 °Fahrenheit)

Summer court
(transition space)

Section

Longitudinal section

St. Andrews Institute of Technology and Management: Girls' Hostel Block

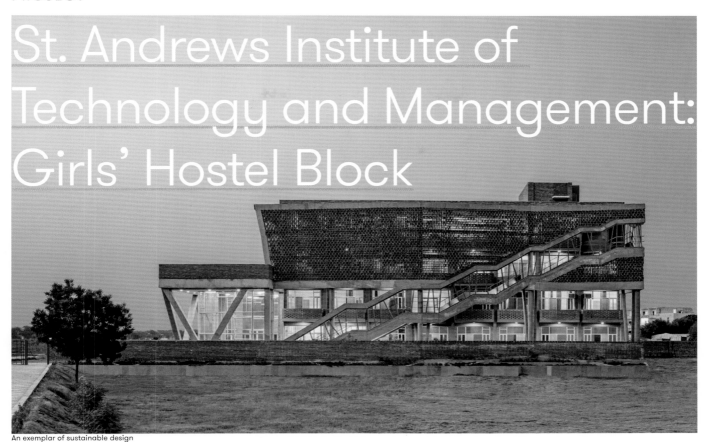

An exemplar of sustainable design

Architect firm: Zero Energy Design Lab (ZED Lab)
Principal architect: Sachin Rastogi and Payal Rastogi
Design team: Rohan Mishra, Naveen Pahal, Shivangi Banerjee
Location: Gurugram, India
Area: 2,323 square meters
Completion date: December 2020
Photography: Noughts and Crosses | Andre J. Fanthome

The girls' hostel block at St. Andrews Institute of Technology and Management in Gurugram explores the intersection of education and sustainability through the lens of the vernacular. Completed in 2020, the design for the 2,323-square-meter girls' hostel takes cues from the adjacent boys' hostel and is articulated in brick and fair-faced concrete, with exposed structural members abutting the structure along all sides. The hostel's design empowers students with the freedom of movement, within an environment that prioritizes thermal comfort and functionality to become an exemplar of a zero-energy design.

The hostel is home to approximately 130 students, with dorm rooms spread across four levels, in addition to hosting ancillary spaces like a pantry, recreational areas, and social spaces. The ground floor comprises twelve double-occupancy rooms along with a double-height reception, pantry, and indoor activity lounge where students can organize gatherings and social events.

Client Brief and Challenges

The design faced a series of challenges from conception to execution. The primary design challenge was to create a secure hub for the girls—a campus within a campus that fit into the urban master plan, and which did not restrict movement, while establishing a connection with the outdoors.

In response to the constraints, the layout has been designed to incorporate indoor and outdoor spaces that connect physically and visually at different levels, to enhance interactions and social activities. To bring in the exterior landscape as part of the building, the entrance foyer and lobby are designed as outdoor spaces to face west, and are connected to the pantry, so that students can enjoy their evenings outside with a spill-out into the green landscape. The students are given the freedom to create their own space in a safe environment without any imposed restrictions.

In terms of construction, too, the staircase and the attached façade posed a design challenge. The free-standing façade was to be constructed at a 30-foot distance from the building, spanning a height of three floors, while keeping in mind structural integrity and earthquake resistance. This was

brought to life through an extensive scaffolding and casting process.

Design and Planning

The design seeks to reinterpret conventional standards of human comfort through the idea of adaptive comfort—which is the principle that each person experiences differently and adapts to a certain extent and variety of indoor conditions, depending on their clothing, their activity, and general physical condition. The building unfolds as a series of multidimensional spaces, arranged in a hierarchical order through the method of adaptive layering. Each space is conceptualized as an intimate environment that prioritizes both functionality and human comfort.

As students move from the interiors of the building into the open, they experience distinct transitions in varying thermal environments. The activity lounge on the ground floor is placed next to the landscaped court. The lounge creates an intimate environment for studying or conversation. Further, the adjacent internal landscaped court features dense plantation to reduce heat gain through evaporative cooling. From the core of the building toward the outdoor, the next transition is at the second-floor terrace along the building's west façade, which attracts students in the mornings and in late evenings in summer; it also serves as an all-day space to congregate during winter.

The design of the building is kept simple while identifying essential elements, such as staircases, informally used as hubs for social interaction. The subsequent transitional zone at the heart of the building is a staircase, aesthetically incorporated into the south façade and connecting all the floors. Transitional and circulation spaces such as bridges open into lounges and pause points, to create room for socializing and group study. Since the bridges create a visual connection, they enhance interaction and interconnection. They seamlessly extend into the student lounges on multiple floors, creating fluid spaces. The staircase manifests as the fundamental social nucleus that is home to all activities, from large-scale celebrations and events, to quick informal conversations. The exterior lobby area often serves as a badminton court in the evenings, and the courtyard that hosts the frequent game of carrom is a space that encourages other similar games and sports.

The Double-skin Façade
With limited space available along the northern façade of the hostel, a double-skin façade is developed with the intention of creating a semi-permeable layer that will help in shading and regulating the temperature between the exterior and interior environments via controlled airflow.

The parametric screen takes cues from the previously developed façade that spans the adjacent boys' hostel within the institute. The façade of the boys' hostel is designed as an envelope in which the rotational angles of the brick were calculated, in order to block diffused and direct radiation. However, over time, it became evident that the depth of the brick, when rotated, was not able to create a deep enough enclosure to cut off diffused radiation in the required manner. So, for the girls' hostel, the exterior façade screen uses hollow pigmented concrete blocks to resemble the color of the red brick; the blocks have been successful in addressing three concerns. Not only do they provide adequate thermal mass to absorb the heat, but with a depth of around 20 centimeters, direct radiation has to penetrate through several layers within the block and, in turn, gets reflected on different surfaces multiple times before entering the interior, reducing glare. In addition, since the block is penetrable, the air volume passing through this mass loses its heat through compression, on the basis of Bernoulli's principle. The blocks are also slightly rotated at a specific angle, based on the insulation analysis, with respect to solar heat gain.

The interior second skin provides a volume where the user can step out to a shaded environment such as a balcony or court. It is a space that prioritizes thermal comfort through the adaptive behavior of the building, and also enables functionality. The second skin takes on the role of a breakout space, such as a terrace, between the interior and exterior. It empowers students to take charge of their environment and activity, and connect with nature while still being inside the building.

Materiality and Architectural Details
The building's materialization in concrete and brickwork binds the different floors together. The columns are round in shape to enhance visual appearance, as well as physicality. Moreover, instead of employing singular columns, the sheer mass is broken down into three columns in a tripod-like configuration to provide better structural stability as a vertical support. The pergola on the roof is designed using cement board and steel beams to achieve a lightweight construction and optimal design quality.

Landscape Strategies and Water Management
The landscape design enriches the space by bringing the greenery inside to serve not only aesthetic, but also functional purposes. Being closer to nature has been scientifically proven to have a favorable impact on psychological and physiological well-being; this also creates a conducive environment for interaction and directs the design's landscape strategy. The edge details of the planters are designed as seaters, allowing students to sit with nature. The shaded courtyard hosts a diverse variety of plant species which require less sun and the peripheral areas feature a bamboo plant screen. Outside the building, where the ground is completely exposed to the sun, champa trees have been planted, selected for their large canopies, to create shaded seating spaces.

The surface of the outdoor landscaped court is penetrable, facilitating ground water penetration. Wastewater from the washrooms is conveyed to the sewage treatment plant and is reused for horticulture.

Sustainability and Energy Efficiency
The girls' hostel building is an exemplar in sustainability through its energy-efficient design. The double-skin façade acts as a thermal mass, reducing direct and diffused radiation on the principal façade by 70 percent, thus minimizing heat gain within the habitable spaces behind the block wall. This further reduces the mechanical cooling loads by 35 percent, a marked increment from the ECBC (Energy Conservation Building Code) base requirement for public buildings.

Materialization in brick and concrete

Bridges and corridors forge connections

Transitional spaces

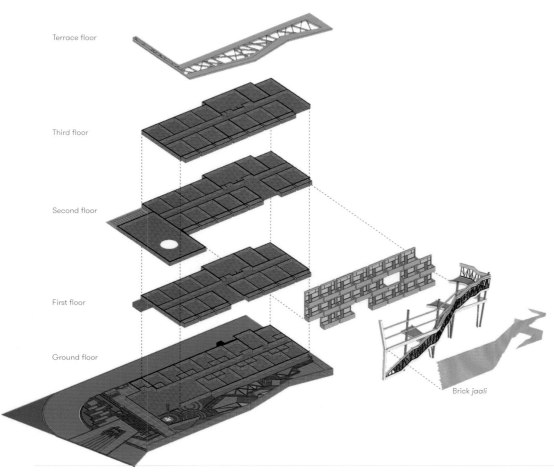

Terrace floor

Third floor

Second floor

First floor

Ground floor

Brick *jaali*

Final axonometric diagram

Interesting play of light and shadow

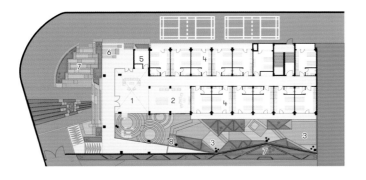

Ground-floor plan

1. Double-height reception
2. Recreational area
3. Landscape court
4. Rooms
5. Pantry
6. Outdoor sitting area
7. Landscape
8. Stairs

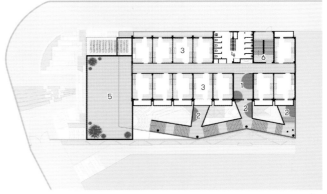

First-floor plan

1. Lounge
2. Connecting bridges
3. Rooms
4. Restrooms
5. Terrace
6. Stairs

N

Night view

Rotated concrete blocks cut radiation

Double-skin hollow concrete block façade

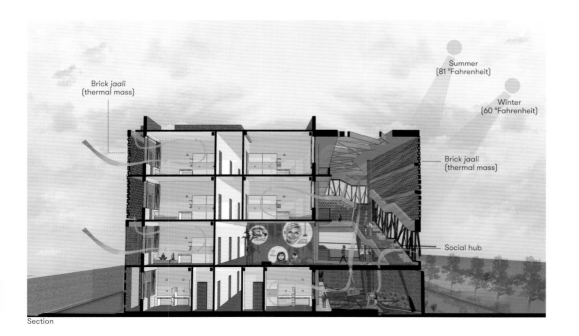

Brick *jaali*
(thermal mass)

Summer
(81 °Fahrenheit)

Winter
(60 °Fahrenheit)

Brick *jaali*
(thermal mass)

Social hub

Section

VORA (Vorasombat Plaza)

View of the office building from the opposite cliff

Architect firm: SPACE | STORY | STUDIO
Principal architect: Pipol Likanapaisal
Design team: Tatiya Chuenpreecha
Location: Bangkok, Thailand
Area: 3,000 square meters
Completion date: 2018
Photography: Chaovarith Poonphol,
Nattakit Jeerapatmaitree

The story began when Piyasombat Property Ltd, the client, acquired a six-story block that forms part of the Vorasombat complex on Rama IV Road. The complex is a joint-block building with two separate entrances—a six-story block on the left and a five-story block on the right. The renovation maintains the existing floor plan based on the structural units and integrates the office space with the retail stores, catering to both the needs of the complex and the neighborhood.

The design executes a "Siamese twins" concept in the new façade, replicating the street-facing front of the two blocks, but with visual distinctions rendered through using different color schemes on each. Vertical circulations are concealed behind an aluminum grille skin, while a glass façade showcases the retail stores inside to commuters on the street, as well as the elevated expressway.

The inspiration for the silver and gold color scheme hails from the former name of the building: Vongvanich—which means "expeditious trading." Instead of paint, the use of aluminum grilles with anodized color modernizes the appearance of the complex; E&A Moonlight Silver for the west side (five-story block) and 510 Golden Sand for the east side (six-story block) was selected.

On the aspect of space management, the building has separate entrances and vertical circulations for both blocks. It was a challenge to allocate a dedicated space for a lobby and the solution arrives at a dual-purpose concept that utilizes the elevator space for the reception as well. To provide extra distance on the limited reception area, so as to enable tenants to adjust from the external climate to the internal environment, the elevator hall on every level serves as a transition zone. The aluminum grille is extended to control brightness, as well as blend conditioned air, to help control the temperature of the environment inside.

As it is intended that the renovated building serves both the retail section and the showroom office, the design of the façade considers many possible varieties of store displays. "No-pattern" is the theme of the direction, so as to avoid any pattern mismatch. This "no-pattern" theme manifests in the misalignment of the aluminum grille and the random arrangement of the glass window panels. The elliptical spiral staircase features as the focal point of the façade.

Façade detail

Façade lighting

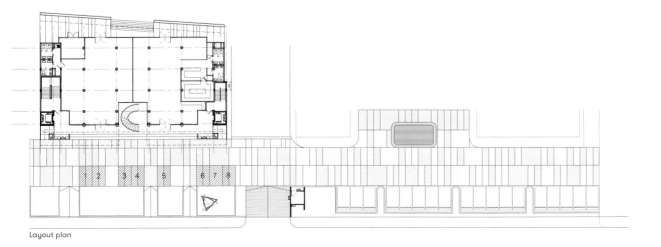

Layout plan

Main entrance

The elliptical spiral stairs is the focal point of the façade

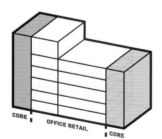

Existing building's spatial arrangement

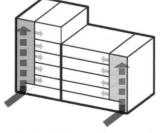

New façade directs circulation upward

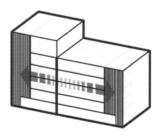

Transitional space is created

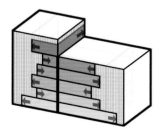

New façade displays a "shifted" design to personalize each floor's retail/office space

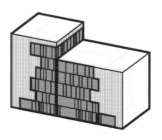

Window sizes are randomized to fit with a variety of window displays

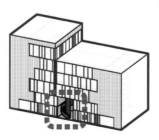

The elliptical staircase focal point connects the whole building and provides circulation to upper floors

Design diagram

Façade between public and rental spaces

Duplex office lobby

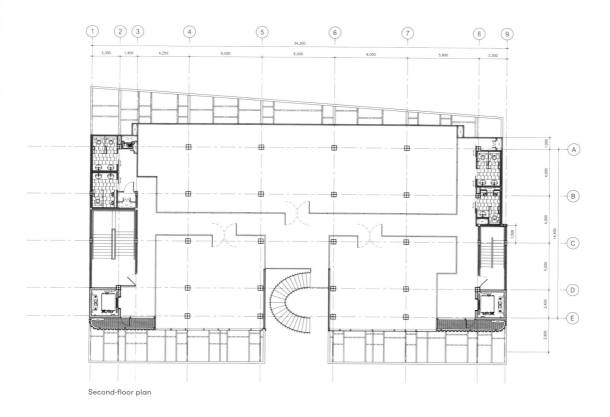

Second-floor plan

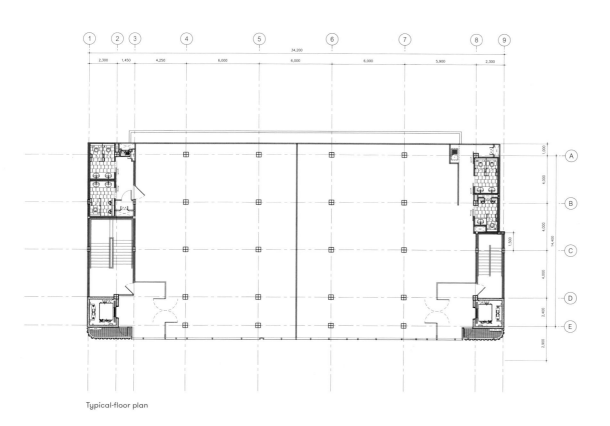

Typical-floor plan

65

Façade detail

Façade detail

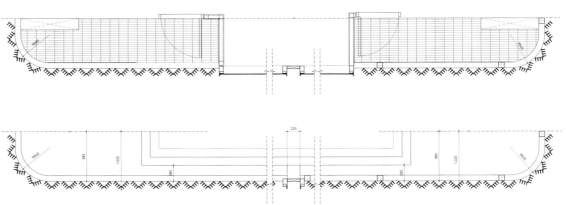

Façade detail plan

The Northstar School

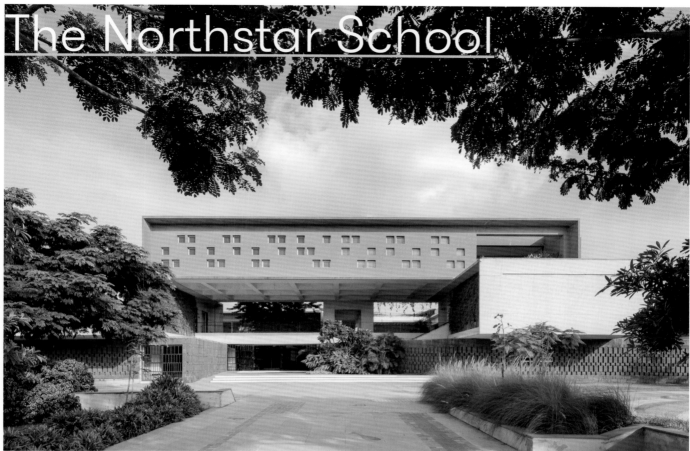

View of the main entry from the pedestrian walkway

Architect firm: Shanmugam Associates
Principal architect: Raja Krishnan, Santhosh Shanmugam, Shanmugam A
Design team: Raja Krishnan, Santhosh Shanmugam, Balasubramanian, Manish Bokdia, Vimala
Location: Rajkot, Gujarat, India
Area: 3,066 square meters
Completion date: 2017
Photography: Ishita Sitwala

"School is an enjoyable and enriching part of life where students can safely explore their true north," reads the vision of The Northstar School, a progressive institution established to transform the education ecosystem.

The client's brief required that a part of every child's experience in Northstar be shaped by architecture. The project sits on the south eastern corner of a 17.8-acre barren site adjoining the RK University campus on Rajkot-Bhavnagar highway.

The semi-arid climate of north-west India, dusty yet windy site conditions, twenty to thirty days of monsoons in Rajkot, and supply of STP (standard temperature and pressure) water from RK University were influential contextual points. The master plan integrates three phases of development; only Phase 1 has been built. Open-ended

corridors, building orientation, and future development were factored into the overall planning. Key functions are situated on the ground and first floors to keep the built space child-friendly.

As the primary intent is to enable ways to learn with nature and the fundamental unit of schools are classrooms, the design process began by programing a single classroom module with cross ventilation, its own private garden, and an open-to-sky *jaali*-fringed courtyard. The module is iterated to arrive from a part to a whole; between two classrooms is a larger garden that has a performance space, with provisions included for conducting classes.

Drawing inspiration from the stepped wells of Gujarat, a central courtyard ties all the spaces within each module, and is replicated in all phases. This central stepped and vegetated courtyard facilitates circulation and serves as a multipurpose space suited for larger gatherings. Integrated within the courtyard, amid green pockets, creepers, and vines, is a stage that is used by children or staff for performances.

With due credit to the structural engineer, the massing on the second floor sits lightly on the floor below and houses a 250-person capacity multipurpose hall. The structure visually creates a presence as one

walks along the heavily canopied main entry walkway.

A secondary skin—*jaalis* at the ground floor and an ambitious creeper screen at the first floor—allows natural light in, shields against dust, and provides privacy. The exploration of material for the façade proceeded along the criteria that it had to be locally available, have an earthy tone, reflect an institutional character, and be economical. Bella, a natural hard lime stone in terra cotta color, has been used to blend the built form with its existing surroundings.

Architecture at The Northstar School has been planned such that as the building ages, the landscape adds more life into the space, therefore, taking ownership.

Presently, an Indian owl resides in an unused truncated duct and the gulmohar trees litter a red carpet of leaves at the main pedestrian entry, tying the scenario in with Northstar's horticulture program that educates its students on the importance of flora and fauna. The design foundations at Northstar lean on the ideologies of exploring contemporary design with local material, using regional references to define the built form, and finding simplistic solutions for complex design problems.

The first-floor classrooms have creepers as a secondary skin that filter and diffuse direct sunlight entering the rooms

Site plan

1. School entry
2. Central plaza
3. Proposed auditorium
4. Plaza
5. Central walkway
6. Main campus entry
7. Main campus building
8. Junior play area
9. Play area
10. Phase 2 and 3 future expansion
11. Orchard
12. Pavilion
13. Swimming pool
14. Sports court
15. Future expansion
16. Basketball court
17. Tennis court
18. Volleyball court
19. Sand pit
20. Skating rink
21. Tree court
22. Bus stop
23. Security cabin
24. RK University entrance
25. Plaza

The cantilevered first-floor classrooms are planned this way to create a shaded play area for the floor below

Cantilevered first-floor classrooms create shaded play areas together with planted shrubs and vegetation

Treated STP water effectively offers nourishment to the green landscape, evident from the lush trails of the climbers that have taken over the corridor areas

Classrooms have their own garden pockets, which can be used as an outdoor venue for lessons

Mesh – a secondary skin for the green creepers that helps reduce harsh sunlight, but allows enough light into the classroom

Locally available kota stone flooring

A 5-foot cantilever provides shade for the ground floor; the cantilever also accommodates a planter box for creepers on the first floor

Large aluminum windows – an insulating material, and act as a thermal barrier

Locally available natural bella stone as a secondary skin for the premises acts as a security barrier and shields against strong winds and harsh light

Isometric view

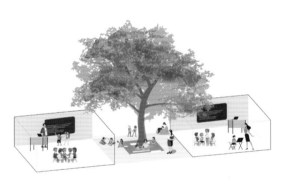

Classrooms formed around a courtyard

Teacher conducting a class in the garden, in the style of older, simpler teaching methods of the past in the villages

An ongoing virtual class is in session in this courtyard, offering relief, especially during the tough times of the pandemic

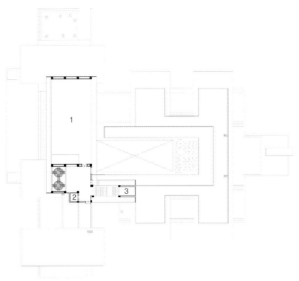

Second-floor plan

1. Seminar hall
2. Elevator
3. Water tank

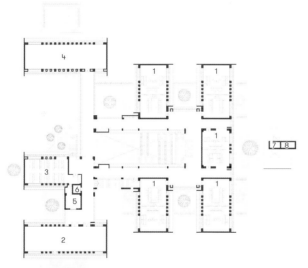

First-floor plan

1. Classroom
2. Performance room
3. Computer lab
4. Lab
5. Server room
6. Elevator
7. Motor room
8. Water tank

Ground-floor plan

1. Reception
2. Waiting area
3. Head of Department room
4. Director
5. Pantry
6. Library
7. Meeting
8. Staff room
9. Classroom
10. Central courtyard
11. Outdoor activity area
12. Restrooms
13. Elevator
14. EB panel room

N
0 1 5   10m

Private gardens have been provided for all spaces, including the library area

Basic shapes and forms are introduced as a part of the architecture

Elevation

Tibet Intangible Cultural Heritage Museum

The museum, river valley, and Potala Palace

Architect firm: Shenzhen Huahui Design Co., Ltd
Principal architect: Xiao Cheng
Design team: Liao Guowei, Liang Ziyi, Zhu Lin, Xu Mu
Location: Lhasa, Tibet, China
Area: 8,000 square meters
Completion date: 2018
Photography: Yao Li

The project is located south of Lhasa, Tibet, with an elevation of nearly 4,000 meters, and gazes upon Potala Palace in the north, while leaning into Potala Mountain in the south. The terrain drops gently from south to north, and can be seen clearly from the whole Lhasa Valley and Potala Palace. The whole project consists of a museum—with a floor area of about 8,000 square meters—and an exhibition garden—with a floor area of 40,000 square meters. The intangible cultural Heritage Museum is the main building, with exhibition halls, courtyards, theaters, offices, an open rooftop, observation halls, and other functional spaces.

In order to better showcase the cultural heritage in Tibet, the unique space concept of Tibet—Heavenly Road—was selected as the origin of the design. Stepping into the museums and parks, one discovers such a "heavenly road," where they can experience the "sky road," which is associated with the natural environment and feel "man's road," which is associated with the building space, heritage treasures, and national culture. As it turns, climbs, and alternates between brightness and darkness to face Potala Palace, "man's road" achieves clarity and intangibility. This path closely integrates the grandness of Potala Palace, the inside of Jokhang Temple, and the abundance of Norbulingka. Walking along the roads and among the monuments, one witnesses a colorful, grand spectacle of life on the Tibetan land, summed up in the forest and vegetation, a theater, terraced gardens, a miniature landscape, festival promenades, and a meditation water courtyard. Meandering with "sky road," the Tibetan culture is wonderfully played back in a modern way.

The museum in the morning mist

Looking over to Potala Palace

Building and the river valley

"Heavenly road" is based on the zigzag
footpath of Potala Palace

Generating "heavenly road"

It forms a spatial circulation from the
entrance of the site to the building, and
spirals up inside the museum

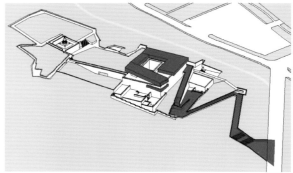

"Heavenly road" combines with the functional space to create a diversified
spatial experience between people and the building

Close-up view

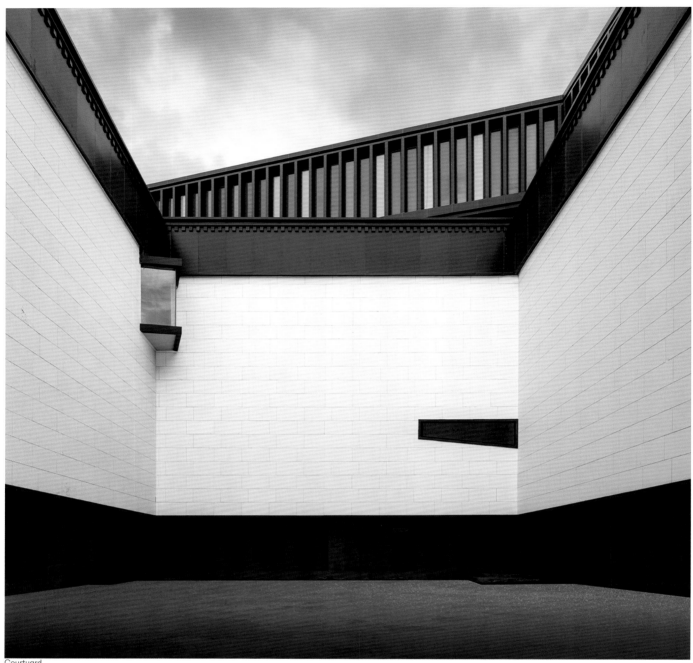

Courtyard

Indoor ramp

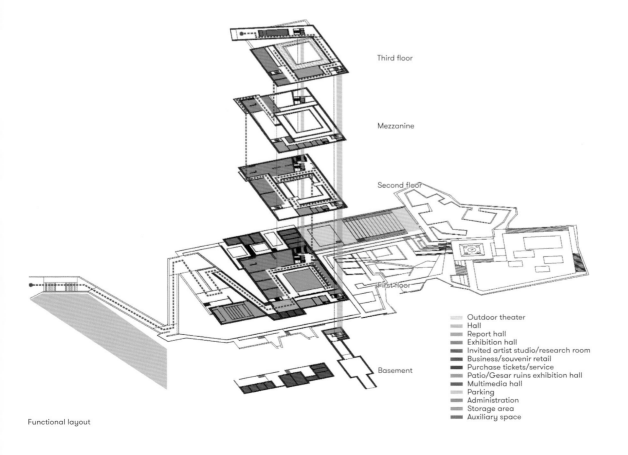

Third floor

Mezzanine

Second floor

First floor

Basement

Outdoor theater
Hall
Report hall
Exhibition hall
Invited artist studio/research room
Business/souvenir retail
Purchase tickets/service
Patio/Gesar ruins exhibition hall
Multimedia hall
Parking
Administration
Storage area
Auxiliary space

Functional layout

Lobby

Exhibition chamber

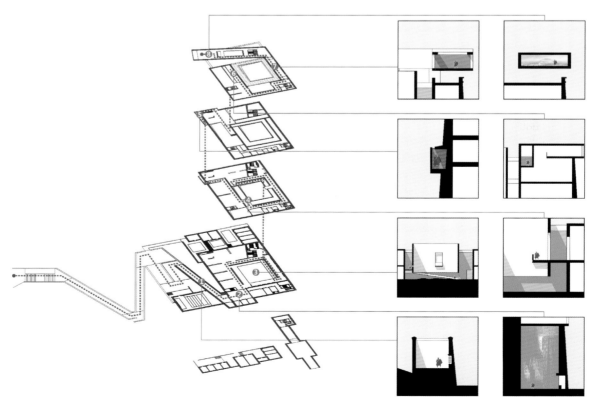

Space experience

Majiabang Cultural Museum

View of the hall from the field

Architect firm: Tongji Architectural Design (Group) Co. Ltd
Principal architect: Zeng Qun
Design team: Wu Min, Li Rongrong
Location: Majiabang Cultural Site, Majiabang Village, Chengnan Street, Nanhu District, Jiaxing City, Zhejiang Province, China
Area: 7840.6 square meters
Completion date: April 2019
Photography: Zhang Yong

The Majiabang culture was a Neolithic culture in the lower reaches of the Yangtze River area in China. Its name comes from the Majiabang archaeological site in Tiandaqiao Village, Nanhu Town, Jiaxing City, Zhejiang Province, where traces of a primitive settlement dating back 7,000 years were discovered. It is known as the "origin of south Yangtze River culture." The Majiabang Cultural Museum is located in Jiaxing City, Zhejiang Province, China, adjacent to the 7,000-year-old prehistoric cultural site.

As a basic unit of analysis in archaeological research, the settlement is an important concept. A settlement is a spatio-temporal archetype composed of fragments of prehistoric civilization that form a readable body comprising countless pieces of historical information. The model of the basic settlement unit, constituted by social relationships and a particular spatial structure built by the Majiabang archaeological team, was adopted as a reference for the idea of a settlement in developing the project concept.

Over the course of the project design, through the reorganization of the original settlement lifestyle found in the Majiabang cultural site, a tacit understanding of this distant civilization across time and space was developed. By taking into consideration the vast original wilderness and water resources retained in the site, the building—which has the same texture as the site—was designed to hide in the environment in a low-key manner, thus showing respect for the surrounding environment. Through a series of visiting circulations, a garden space is formed along traditional Chinese architectural spaces.

The fifth façade, which is formed of organic geometric units, has an intertextual relationship with the "jigsaw" of fields crisscrossing the surrounding area, and the undulating, sloping roof provides a spatial experience akin to sheltering under the original shacks. The museum's public spaces follow the path between the "huts," and is entered via a corner courtyard that creates an entry point into the original space, giving it a sense of history. The physical manipulation of the building abstracts the prototype of the settlement, leaving a considerable amount of blank space in the geometric combination process. The spatial connections of the real and the virtual form an image of the settlement as "house and courtyard interlaced," which corresponds to the traditional Jiangnan lifestyle in the Jiaxing area.

A viewing platform has been built at the end of the tour path, attracting visitors

to the site, with an interest to get closer to history and "touch" the past.

The Majiabang Cultural Museum uses a mixture of terra cotta and pigmented concrete as the main material for its façade. The clay color of the fair-faced concrete is inspired by the historical fragments of pottery unearthed on the site; it is realized using organic convex and concave wooden molds, to create the impression of containing an ancient civilization by reproducing its original ecological texture. Over the course of a day, sunlight creates vivid expressions on the surface of the museum.

Passive energy-saving techniques have been adopted for the museum, taking full advantage of the natural lighting and ventilation. The building uses solar photovoltaic systems and energy-efficient equipment, providing energy-efficient lighting and intelligent control technology. A high-strength glass curtain wall system (including a full glass curtain wall) is also used in the building.

Aiming to be a first-class museum with international influence, the Majiabang Cultural Museum displays the long history of the Majiabang culture and serves to bring an element of scientific knowledge and education to the public. The exhibition takes Jiaxing as its center, comprehensively displaying the archaeological culture and cultural influence of Majiabang around Tai Lake, which reaches the north bank of the Qiantang River in Zhejiang in the south, and Changzhou in Jiangsu in the northwest.

Bird's-eye view

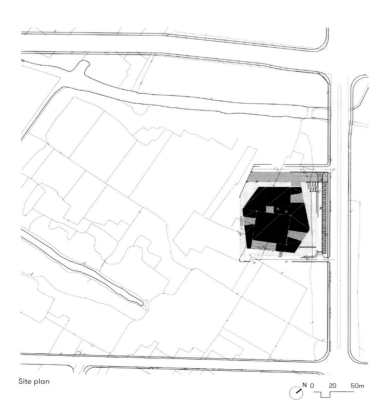

Site plan

N 0   20   50m

Form generation analysis

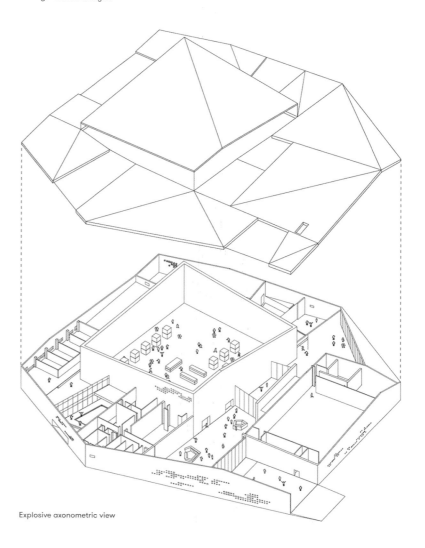

Explosive axonometric view

View of the cultural ruins and the museum

View of the courtyard with water

View of the courtyard

View of the courtyard from inside

View of the interior and skylight

1. Courtyard
2. Hall
3. Meeting room
4. Exhibition room
5. Temporary exhibition room
6. Café
7. Education development corner
8. Acquisitions and reservations
9. Display and exhibition
10. Education and publicity
11. Cultural study center
12. Staff's rest quarters
13. Restroom
14. Control center
15. Restaurant
16. Reference collection
17. Relic obervation room
18. Equipment room

N   0   5   20   30m

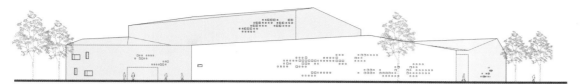

Elevation

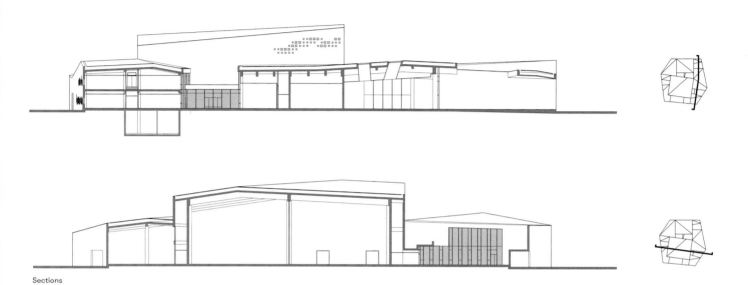

Sections

View of the entrance

Visitor Center of Changping Future Science City

The rear of the visitor center

Architect firm: Huyue Studio
Principal architect: Hu Yue
Design team: Hu Yue, Tai Fangqing, Lv Chao, Xiang Xi, Wang Xixi, Jiang Yang, Liu Yang, Lu Dongyang, Zhang Cheng, Pei Lei
Location: Changping District, Beijing, China
Area: 874 square meters
Completion date: 2018
Photography: Chen Su

The project is the Visitor Center located at the main entrance to Central Park in Changping, which is located in a large industrial park on the outskirts of Beijing. The park is built where an old river used to course through, and it incorporates a central lake area, based on a river course that was formed during early site planning. During construction, it was noticed that small service facilities and landscape design that had been planned for looked unnatural and conflicted with the environment, so some changes were initiated as the build progressed.

The main entrance is located on the south side of the park, close to the city expressway in the south. Across the urban expressway is a dense construction area; like many new development zones in China, villages originally occupying the site have been relocated, and modern buildings and wide streets are being constructed. The Visitor Center is located at the junction of the construction site and the park.

Before the project commenced, the landscape planning team had already come up with a plan for the Visitor Center. The plan adopted a gate design with a catering facility above the entrance. The image of a gate-like structure is familiar and popular among people, and also meets the expectation of the client for a landmark entrance. However, such a design would have a negative impact on the natural environment; and it was the architects' top priority to design an environmentally friendly Visitor Center. The square in front of the park's main entrance has a height difference of 6 meters from the lake. This height difference has been used to conceal the building in the environment, thereby achieving desirable results.

Two arc-shaped ramps that extend from the front square to both sides, along the two rows of trees preserved on the east and west sides of the Visitor Center, were designed. The ramps extend all the way, from the front square to the lake, and the Visitor Center is located between the two ramps. From the park entrance, square stairs descend and lead visitors to the Visitor Center.

In layout, the Visitor Center represents a breakthrough—compared to the previous design of having multiple functions in one space—by dividing the space into two parts. One part is located under the west ramp and includes restrooms and changing rooms, and the other part is located on the east side and is a glass-enclosed space with an information desk, café, supermarket, computer room, and offices. Between the two structures is a spacious passage, which leads directly from the park entrance square to the lake. Looking from the lake to the Visitor Center, blocked by the east and west ramps and big trees, you can only see two concrete walls separating the flow of people, and a stand built according to the terrain. In this way, the Visitor Center is fully integrated with the natural environment and the flow of people, forming a natural landscape characterized by minimal intervention.

The project started with the idea of coordinating human-made objects and the natural environment, and evolves to break the geometric boundary between traditional buildings and the external environment by fully integrating the two. The building is embedded into the landform with a low-profile design, creating a novel architectural landscape. Abandoning the strong contrast between new buildings and an environment of the past, it foregrounds the design paradigm of sculpture-like buildings. At the same time, the simple and efficient geometrical design inside the Visitor Center properly expresses the traditional values of modernist architecture. More importantly, it makes city managers realize that environmentally friendly buildings and de-marked buildings are the way of the future.

The entryway, seen from the roof terrace

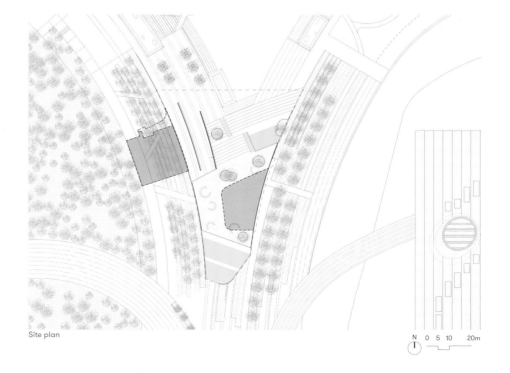

Site plan

N   0 5 10   20m

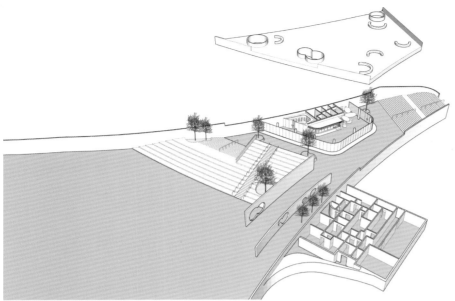

First-floor plan, axonometric drawing

Main stairs

Stairs on the north side

Stairs and access to the north side

North entrance

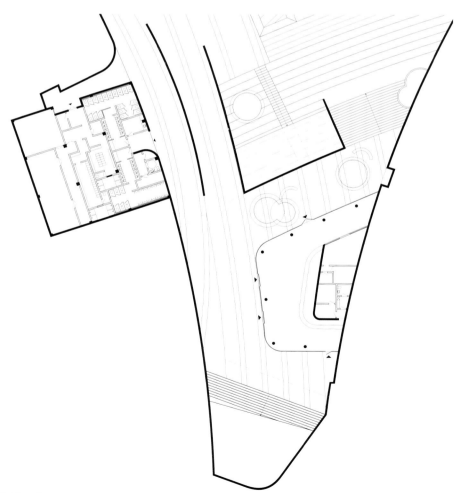

First-floor plan

Night view

Café area of the Visitor Center

Detail

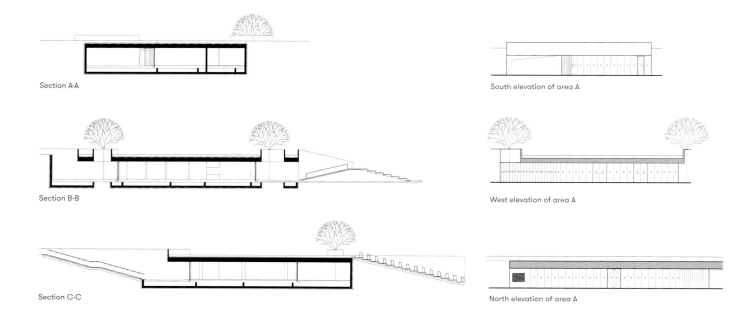

Section A-A

South elevation of area A

Section B-B

West elevation of area A

Section C-C

North elevation of area A

View from the main square

East side view

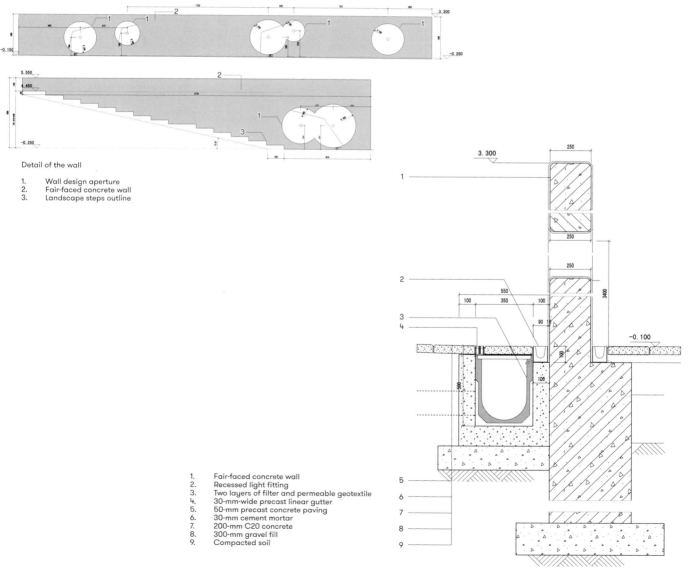

Detail of the wall

1. Wall design aperture
2. Fair-faced concrete wall
3. Landscape steps outline

1. Fair-faced concrete wall
2. Recessed light fitting
3. Two layers of filter and permeable geotextile
4. 30-mm-wide precast linear gutter
5. 50-mm precast concrete paving
6. 30-mm cement mortar
7. 200-mm C20 concrete
8. 300-mm gravel fill
9. Compacted soil

Detail of the wall

Morse Park Amphitheatre

Shelter extending into the park

Architect firm: Architectural Services Department, HKSARG
Principal architect: Alice Yeung, Thomas Wan
Design team: Tuesday Li, David Leung
Location: Kowloon, Hong Kong, China
Area: 2,369 square meters
Completion date: 2018
Photography: Keith Chan

The site is an existing amphitheater in Morse Park, which was completed in 1967 and has since grown along with the Wong Tai Sin District in Kowloon.

The architects thought carefully about what they could inject into the setting of this aging district in Hong Kong in order to benefit the community, and it was decided that the plan of action would be to regenerate a focus in the midst of the landscape. While preserving the original essence of the park, which has become a part of daily life for the residents, the architects opted to enhance the outdoor theatre for the regular performances of Cantonese operas, and to expand the potential of the venue to attract a variety of activities into the neighborhood.

The open theatre respects the tradition of courtyard performance in Chinese opera history. Performances of different natures are encouraged within a wide range of activities, ranging from operas to park concerts, as well as "share & care" events, and weekend bazaars.

The concept regenerates a focus on the park by creating and connecting a variety of spaces to encourage diversified activities. On entering the forecourt (through the park), a metal trellis with a small bamboo patch guides to the pavilion on one side; an extending canopy indicates the amphitheater on the other. The amphitheater shelter stretches into the park greenery, merging the structure with the surrounding park. The flow of the shelter unites the amphitheater with its surroundings, and performers with their participants. Different elements come together in a dynamic whole, juxtaposed between old and new, and balancing between geometrical purity and the natural environment, creating multiple layers of space for individual wandering and casual gatherings for organized social events. The trellis, shelter, and greenery create a variety of spatial experiences. While preserving the daily routines of the residents, diversified activities are brought into this neighborhood park, fostering communication between different generations.

The existing park and amphitheater are enhanced to accommodate current-day events, allowing the sustainable development of the amphitheater, as well as the park, such that they continue their growth with the district. While providing shelter over the amphitheater and the seating, the sides of the venue are kept open to let in natural light and ventilation. A skylight is introduced in the canopy over the amphitheater to create a focus on the central performance area and enhance the effect of natural daylight. Vertical greening, together with metal canopies and trellis, act as shading, while creating a natural setting. The surrounding park greenery and vertical greening allow natural scenery into the amphitheater, providing a harmonious backdrop for the events. The open theater provides an energy-friendly alternative as a performance and event ground that also lends the magical experience of watching a "show" within a natural park setting. The theater in the park supports the sustainable growth of the park and the district.

View from forecourt

New entry into the amphitheater

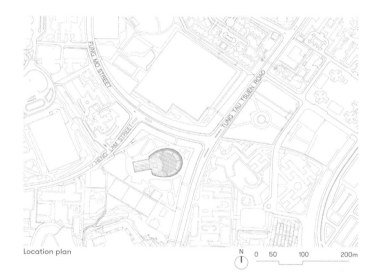
Location plan

N   0   50   100   200m

View to the skylight

Northwest aerial view

Open space outside the pavilion

The amphitheater

Extended shelter merging with nature

View along trellis and bamboo patch

Night view of the pavilion

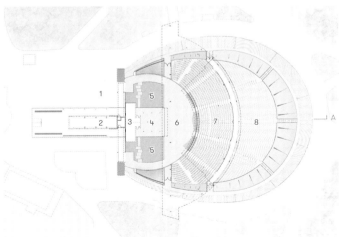

Ground-floor plan

1. Forecourt
2. Pavilion
3. Dressing room
4. Deck
5. Lawn
6. Main stage
7. Seating area
8. Existing amphitheater seats
9. Metal shelter
10. Skylight
11. Seat shelter

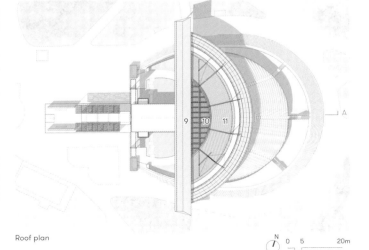

Roof plan

N 0 5 20m

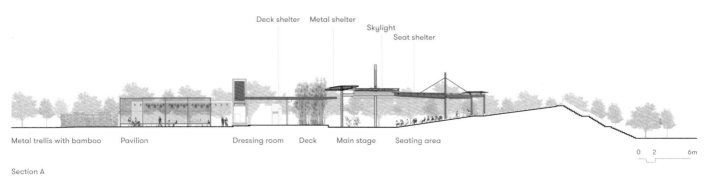

Deck shelter   Metal shelter

Skylight

Seat shelter

Metal trellis with bamboo   Pavilion   Dressing room   Deck   Main stage   Seating area

0   2   6m

Section A

Striated House at Rajagiriya

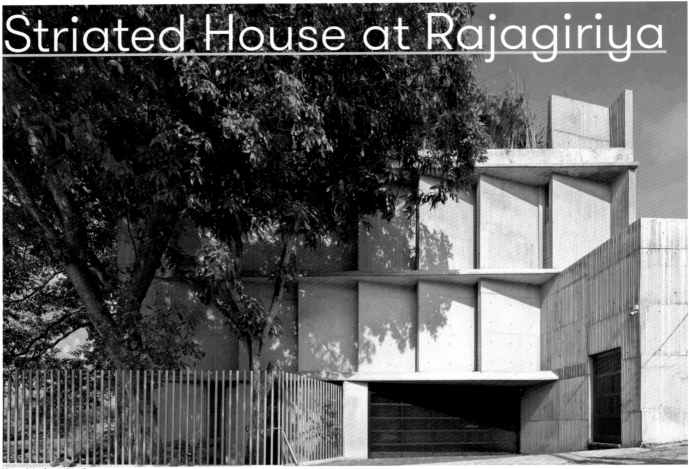

View of the front elevation

Architect firm: Palinda Kannangara Architects
Principal architect: Palinda Kannangara
Structural engineer: Shiromal Femando
Landscape design: Varna Shashidhar
Location: Rajagiriya, Sri Lanka
Area: 504 square meters
Completion date: 2019
Photography: Ganindu Balasuriya

Located in a fairly dense suburb of Colombo, Sri Lanka, the striated house is a family home that sits facing a marsh, surrounded by taller buildings on three sides. The windows are orientated toward, and completely open up to the marsh and the north. The western façade, which faces the street is stolid with fins; it's a façade that gives little away to a rather dense neighborhood filled with three- and four-floor buildings, and even taller buildings beyond. The home is built on a site of 1,765 square meters.

Entering the home is a journey: from the outside world, through a narrow space, reminiscent of a calming "portal" (entryway) in spiritual spaces; from a busy street into a more private realm. The exteriors of the walls are cast in light that hits the surface directly in some parts, and filters through a tree in other parts, creating a beautiful shadow portrait of nature on the façade; a slender stairwell, dramatically lit, culminates at the fish pond at the upper most level. The first floor comprises the living spaces, painted with capturing views, and guestrooms, and a staircase that leads down. The entire ground floor opens out.

The concrete fins occupy the entire western façade, while the main house faces north and the marsh, providing the living area with panoramic views. The ground level situates the dining area, kitchen, and facilities. The helper's space is connected to the garage and back garden, with direct access from the parking court.

The second floor is the most intimate, comprising of the main bedroom, the children's bedrooms, and a family room with a wide balcony, into which living spaces can extend; this space can be used year-round. The uppermost level makes up the lounge pavilion, complete with a bar. Set between treetops, it invites beautiful panoramic views of the wetland outside and bird life.

The design makes use of its sloping site, creating a home which maximizes the levels and views of the surrounding area. The material palette is simple; only the fin wall is made of slender concrete and follows the site boundary. The rest of the building is composed of brick walls, promoting the creative use of materials in the tropics. The rooftop is an intensive green roof that is totally permeable, made out of locally available crushed laterite aggregate "borelu." A biological pond that is filled with freshwater fish, tall reeds, and water lilies screens off the neighboring high-rises, providing privacy to the interior; it also regulates storm water. The rooftop aids cooling with solar panels, ensuring that the air conditioner can remain off almost year-round.

The trees and gardens are added shading elements to the home, as shadow and shade are essential to tropical living. The kitchen garden is home to fruit trees and herbs used in daily cooking, which include banana trees and turmeric plants, among other varieties. This has been most useful, especially during the difficult pandemic times, when the family has been living and working from their retreat-like home.

The home promotes self-reliance and sustainability, while maintaining a contemporary approach to tropical architecture and the exploration of materials.

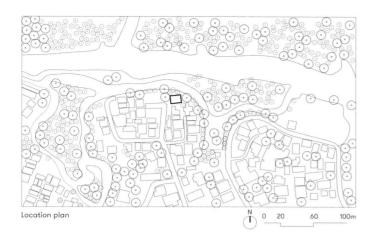

Location plan

N
0 20 60 100m

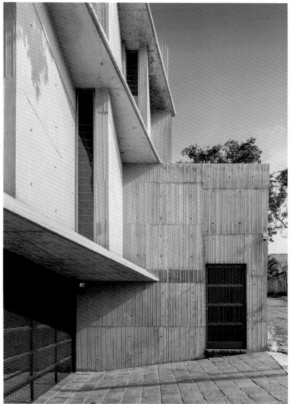

View of the front entrance

View of the living room

View of the double-height dining area

View of the rooftop entertainment pavilion

View of the bedroom

View of the double-height entrance court

View of the double-height dining area

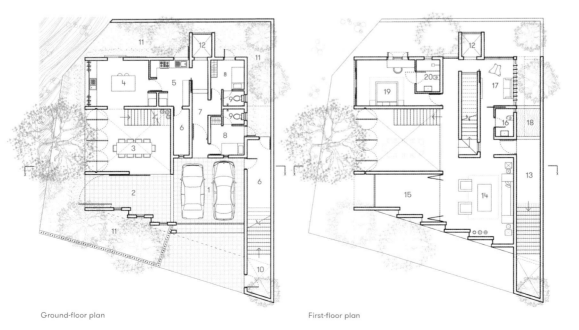

Ground-floor plan

First-floor plan

1. Parking
2. Outdoor paved area
3. Dining area
4. Pantry
5. Kitchen
6. Store room
7. Service passage
8. Helper's room
9. Helper's bathroom
10. Entrance court
11. Garden
12. Elevator
13. Entrance
14. Living room
15. Balcony
16. Powder room
17. TV room
18. Pond
19. Bedroom
20. Bathroom
21. Family room
22. Main bedroom
23. Main bathroom
24. Dressing room
25. Shrine/altar
26. Utility room
27. Open-to-sky courtyard
28. Pavilion
29. Rooftop bar
30. Rooftop garden

View of the balcony from the living area

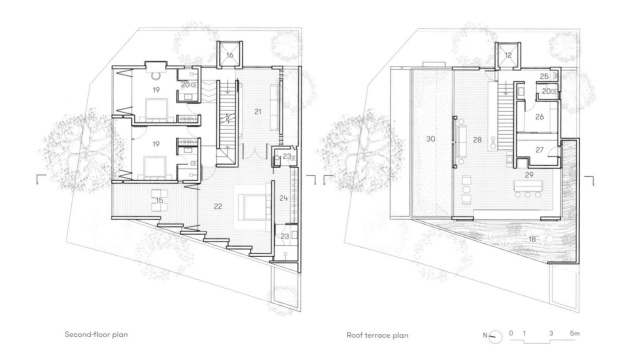

Second-floor plan

Roof terrace plan

N   0   1   3   5m

View of the rooftop terrace

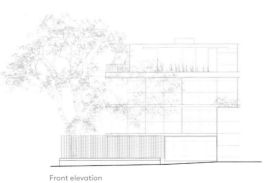

Front elevation

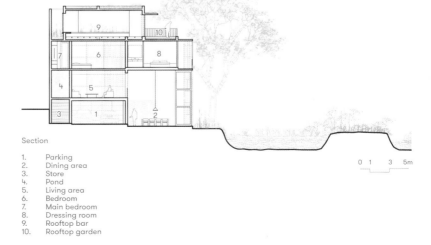

Section

1.   Parking
2.   Dining area
3.   Store
4.   Pond
5.   Living area
6.   Bedroom
7.   Main bedroom
8.   Dressing room
9.   Rooftop bar
10.   Rooftop garden

Xi'an International Convention and Exhibition Center (Cooperative Design, in partnership with gmp and WES)

TJAD employs more than five thousand outstanding architectural design and engineering personnel to provide top engineering consulting services for our clients, and we have been working hard to promote urban development, so that we may build a better life for citizens through our many professional practices.

We firmly believe that it is the trust that our clients have in us that gives TJAD opportunities to grow. As part of the society and industry, we strive to continue to channel unremitting efforts toward industry development and social progress, just like we have been doing the past sixty-four years.

Contingency and Temporary Medical Building of Shanghai Public Health Clinical Center

Shangyin Opera House (Cooperative Design, in partnership with Christian de Portzamparc, Xu-Acoustique, and Theater Projects Consultants)

Green Hill, Shanghai

TONGJI ARCHITECTURAL DESIGN (GROUP) CO., LTD. (TJAD)

VISION

Become a respected design and engineering consultancy with global influence

MISSION

Enable people to live and work in a better place with our creative labor

CORE VALUES

Focus on customers and grow together with employees

SPIRIT

Work together and pursue excellence

Address: No.1230 Siping Road, Shanghai, China, 200092
Telephone: 0086-21-65987788
Email: 5wjia@tjad.cn
Web: www.tjad.cn